Multimedia English Textbook
for Intermediate Learners

Jooyoung Yoon

VOX ENGLISH

Watching YouTube, you can learn key English expressions in major fields with fun.

Hi English

Published by	Jooyoung Yoon
Edited by	Hongsik Lim
First Issued on	August 15, 2024
Phone Number	(02) 335 1002
Fax	(02) 6499 0219
Address	Korea, Seoul, Mapo-gu, Hongik-ro 5an-gil 8 3F
Homepage	www.hienglish.com
E-mail	jay@hienglish.com
Price	KRW 25,000
ISBN Number	979-11-85342-35-1

No Unauthorized Photocopying

The video content referenced in this book is owned by VOX Media, and readers are encouraged to visit the VOX channel on YouTube to watch it.

Copyright © 2024 by HiEnglish. All rights reserved.

No part of this publication may be reproduced, distributed, or transmitted in any form or by any means, including photocopying, recording, or other electronic or mechanical methods, without the prior written permission of the publisher.

VOXENGLISH
Preface

Since 2002, HiEnglish has dedicated itself to corporate foreign language education. Based on our observation of numerous learners abandoning their foreign language studies, we have conducted extensive research on effective learning methods. Previously, the primary focus of foreign language education was exams, but now it has shifted to preparing students for real life and work. To overcome the problem of passive repetitive memorization learning, we found the answer on YouTube, where you can learn foreign languages by watching your favorite video clips.

HiEnglish has introduced VOXEnglish, a platform designed to cater to the needs of busy office workers. This innovative platform allows you to learn English effectively in a shorter amount of time, all while selecting videos that resonate with Koreans. Established in America in 2014, Vox Media offers engaging video content that makes learning English not just a task, but an enjoyable experience.

VOXEnglish has several innovative and unique features. First, unlike other English textbooks that make students simply listen and solve problems, this book focuses on activities so pupils can listen and speak naturally. Second, besides textbook-like topics, you can learn English expressions related to major issues in each field of society while watching rather than studying them. Third, VOX English incorporates vocabulary, fill-in-the-blank exercises, conversational expressions, topic discussions, and quizzes to make learning English enjoyable. Fourth, with 15 10-minute YouTube video clips, you can gradually improve your vocabulary, listening, and speaking skills.

HiEnglish is committed to reigniting your passion for English learning through VOXEnglish. We believe that this platform will not only enhance your English proficiency but also open doors to new opportunities in your personal and professional life. We sincerely hope that more people will use VOXEnglish as a stepping stone to realize their dreams and aspirations.

CEO of HiEnglish
Jooyoung Yoon

TABLE OF CONTENTS

Unit 1.	The Secrets of Airplane Legroom	01
Unit 2.	Ukraine under Siege	07
Unit 3.	Navigating the Trade Highway	13
Unit 4.	Breaking Phone Addiction	19
Unit 5.	The Hidden Dangers of Sliding Sports	25
Unit 6.	Inequality and Climate Change	31
Unit 7.	Artificial Intelligence in Warfare	37
Unit 8.	Impacts of Light on Sleep Cycles	43
Unit 9.	The Secret behind the Shaky Inflation Rate	49
Unit 10.	The Origin of the Word "OK"	55
Unit 11.	The History of Gun Control in Texas	61
Unit 12.	The Colonial Legacy in Jakarta	67
Unit 13.	The New Microchip Cold War	73
Unit 14.	Unveiling Media Deception	79
Unit 15.	From Orchards to Tech Powerhouse	85
Answer		91

UNIT 1 The Secrets of Airplane Legroom

Video title: How airplane legroom got so tight?
This unit is based on the YouTube content as stated above.

> Heads-up

VOCABULARY

Unit | 1

Match the vocabulary on the left with their definitions on the right.

01 seat pitch — **A** the part of the body one sits on

02 buttock — **B** items or services that are grouped or packaged together as a single unit

03 bulkhead seat — **C** a seat located at the partition (bulkhead) between sections of an aircraft

04 bundled together — **D** the space available for a passenger's legs while seated

05 inclined to — **E** tending or likely to do something

06 literally — **F** feeling crowded or lacking space

07 segmentation — **G** the process of dividing a market into distinct groups based on characteristics

08 cramped — **H** the action of tilting or moving a seat backward to increase comfort

09 evacuation — **I** in a literal or exact sense, without exaggeration or metaphor

10 reclining — **J** the organized removal of people from a dangerous area to a safer location

EXPRESSION

Unit | 1

Watch the video and fill in the blanks with correct expressions.

> A that big of B in front of C way back D upright E thereabouts
> F inclined G adjust for H at a cost I back in time J their choice

01 0:33 ~ 0:39

Seat pitch is the fancy term used to describe the distance between where your seat begins and the seat _____ you ends.

02 1:12 ~ 1:13

When I'm sitting down in an _____ position.

03 1:31 ~ 1:35

What's that look like? Five, six inches? Yeah, _____.

04 1:56 ~ 1:57

I'm not _____ a guy.

05 4:51 ~ 4:52

_____ in the day they didn't charge different prices

06 5:21 ~ 5:22

events that made people less _____ to travel.

07 6:09 ~ 6:10

It's not _____ to be tall.

08 6:19 ~ 6:26

and _____ inflation, you can see that compared to 1993 domestic flights have actually gotten less expensive.

09 6:57 ~ 6:58

I think we will not go _____.

10 8:33 ~ 8:39

For now, seat pitch is still up to airlines and comfort still comes _____.

FILL IN THE BLANK

Unit | 1

Watch the video and fill in the blanks with the correct words.

01 0:27 ~ 0:33
As you can see here: economy class which is where I'll be sitting, has a 1._____ between 28 and 30 inches.

02 1:14 ~ 1:31
My buttock-to-knee length which, before you harass me in the comments is the official 2._____ that the FAA use in its testing ends up being about 20 inches. And when I got on this plane... I ended up being fairly comfortable because I have 3._____ between my knee and the seat in front of me.

03 2:19 ~ 2:27
When I watch movies that take place in 50s, 60s, 70s, everything seems so much more 4._____ and 5._____.

04 4:01 ~ 4:16
But I had way more legroom. Not only was I in Economy Plus but I also ended up in the notoriously spacious 6._____. While, yes, I do get extra legroom. I also have a ton of extra responsibility in case this plane 7._____.

05 5:00 ~ 5:14
He coauthored this 2022 paper that examined in-flight 8._____ by carriers provided by the US airlines. In the past everything would be 9._____ in your ticket price. You'd get a 10._____, a bag you usually got to choose your seats.

06 6:37 ~ 6:53
Yeah, that means changing the design of the seats to literally take out 11._____ and depth from your seat back. For many airlines, this 12._____ meant that they were able to add an extra row of seats. But most seats got an inch closer together.

07 6:54 ~ 7:15
For my experience, the seats were pretty comfortable though. I think we will not go back in time where they had one price for wherever you sat in 13._____. I believe what we're going to see is continue 14._____ in the market offering a variety different classes of products... and then allow the consumer to 15._____.

08 7:29 ~ 7:34
if there could be a standard that was less 16._____... I'd be 17._____.

09 7:51 ~ 8:09
The bill was signed into law on October 5th, 2018 but as of 2023, there are still no regulations in part thanks to a March court decision that decided there wasn't enough clear and indisputable evidence that small seats materially slow the exit of passengers 18._____.

10 8:33 ~ 8:50
For now, seat pitch is still up to airlines and comfort still comes 19._____. Once on my honeymoon, I got upgraded to first class so it was quite nice. You can enjoy that but I'm not willing to pay that 20._____.

4 | HiEnglish

Unit | 1

Read the following questions and share your answers in class.

Discussion Question 1

"Boeing is on an airplane with a computer, whereas Airbus is a computer with wings." If the computer checks the pilot's input and exceeds its limits, Airbus will not comply. Airbus analyzed numerous air accidents and determined that human error was the root cause. Boeing, on the other hand, gives pilots greater power. Boeing guarantees pilots more convenience and authority. The pilots can control the aircraft with more confidence and stability. The experienced pilot's handling can be more effective than the computer, especially in unexpected situations.

Which company plane would you like to travel on abroad? What do you think? Why do you think so?

Discussion Question 2

There were several cases in which airlines denied boarding to passengers with autism and overweight individuals due to safety reasons.

Which one should prioritize the right to travel, protected by constitutional rights or safety regulations that sometimes necessitate denying boarding to ensure the safety and comfort of other passengers? What do you think? Why do you think so?

Unit | 1

Watch the part of the video and choose the correct answers.

01 What are the measurements of the current seat pitch in economy class?
- A 28 to 30 inches
- B 30 to 34 inches
- C 35 to 39 inches

02 How many more passengers can be seated in the airplane than in 1936?
- A approximately 30 passengers
- B approximately 150 passengers
- C approximately 180 passengers

03 Why did two individuals feel differently about the legroom?
- A They were traveling on different types of airplanes.
- B They had different amounts of legroom due to varying seat configurations.
- C They were in different classes of service on the same flight.

04 How much legroom was decreased in length?
- A 1 to 4 inches
- B 4 to 8 inches
- C 9 to 12 inches

05 How much did the narrator pay for the premium economy seat?
- A extra 30 dollars
- B extra 50 dollars
- C extra 100 dollars

06 What is the difference between the regular and exit row seats?
- A have extra responsibilities
- B have extra ticket price
- C have extra TV

07 How many different tiers of seats were mentioned in the script?
- A 2 tiers
- B 3 tiers
- C 4 tiers

08 How did the airline make room in the airplane?
- A by designing thinner seats
- B by making the plane bigger
- C by changing the flight to have more seats

09 How did the narrator feel about the current legroom?
- A more than enough
- B enough to travel
- C need more space

10 What is the reason for still not regulating the legroom?
- A still have enough space for the passengers
- B not enough evidence of slowing down the evacuation
- C lobby of the airline company to make money

UNIT 2 Ukraine under Siege

Video title: Putin's war on Ukraine, explained
This unit is based on the YouTube content as stated above.

> Heads-up

VOCABULARY

Unit | 2

Match the vocabulary on the left with their definitions on the right.

01 invasion   **A** people killed or injured in a war or accident

02 shelter   **B** an instance of invading a country or region with an armed force

03 sovereign   **C** the condition of a nation, country, or state which exercises self-government

04 casualties   **D** to protect or shield from harm, danger, or adverse conditions

05 protest   **E** a union or association formed for mutual benefit

06 annex   **F** a nation acting independently and without outside interference

07 overthrow   **G** a statement or action expressing disapproval of or objection

08 independence   **H** to remove forcibly from power

09 alliance   **I** penalties taken by one or more countries to restrict trade and official contacts

10 Economic sanction   **J** to incorporate a territory into another country or state

EXPRESSION

Unit | 2

Watch the video and fill in the blanks with correct expressions.

> **A** spiraled into **B** on standby **C** took to the streets **D** hardened into **E** have broken out
> **F** end in failure **G** bear the consequences **H** at a cost **I** under attack **J** opening their borders

01 0:31 ~ 0:36
All these cities are _____, including the capital of Kyiv which has become Putin's main target.

02 1:36 ~ 1:42
In 1917, the Russian Revolution brought down the empire and the region _____ a civil war.

03 2:23 ~ 2:27
And soon these spheres _____ military alliances.

04 4:16 ~ 4:23
After the decision was announced, hundreds of thousands of protesters _____ to demand the agreement be signed.

05 5:23 ~ 5:29
Satellite images showed at least 100,000 Russian troops and military equipment _____ along the border of Ukraine.

06 5:47 ~ 5:52
Instead, they put forces _____ and reinforced their military presence in Eastern Europe.

07 7:13 ~ 7:18
"This hideous and barbaric venture of Vladimir Putin must _____."

08 7:19 ~ 7:24
"Putin chose this war and now he and his country will _____."

09 7:25 ~ 7:27
Anti-war protests _____ around the world.

10 7:31 ~ 7:35
Neighboring nations have _____ as hundreds of thousands of Ukrainians attempt to flee.

FILL IN THE BLANK

Unit | 2

Watch the video and fill in the blanks with the correct words.

01 1:21 ~ 1:31
But Ukraine is a 1. _____ nation with its own language, culture, and political system. And while the two countries do have a shared history Ukraine has fought hard for its own 2. _____.

02 2:08 ~ 2:22
The Soviet Union installed 3. _____ governments on their side which were easy for them to control. But the west developed into 4. _____ with capitalist economies. The deep ideological divide fueled distrust and tensions between the two sides.

03 2:56 ~ 3:07
By late 1991, republics like Ukraine began 5. _____ from Soviet domination. The Soviet Union dissolved into 15 6. _____ countries, including a much weaker Russia.

04 3:43 ~ 3:56
But Ukraine and Georgia both 7. _____ NATO for a long time. And that made them prime targets for Russia. Ukraine became a NATO partner in 1994 which brought them a step closer to 8. _____.

05 4:50 ~ 5:00
First, he invaded and annexed Ukraine's 9. _____. Then, Russia-backed separatists 10. _____ the regions of Donetsk and Luhansk and declared them independent of Ukraine.

06 5:53 ~ 6:06
Back at Ukraine's border, Russian troops continued to gather. And over here, along its border with Belarus, Russia began 11. _____ huge military drills. On February 21st, the threat of war 12. _____.

07 6:20 ~ 6:27
His troops immediately crossed the 13. _____ into Russian-backed separatist regions under the pretense of peacekeeping. Ukraine announced a 14. _____.

08 6:57 ~ 7:07
Hours later on February 24th, Putin launched a full-scale 15. _____ in Ukraine. World leaders have 16. _____ against Russia's invasion.

09 7:25 ~ 7:36
Anti-war 17. _____ have broken out around the world. Including in Russia, despite the risk of arrest. Neighboring nations have 18. _____ as hundreds of thousands of Ukrainians attempt to flee.

10 8:08 ~ 8:17
So countries around the world are imposing some of the harshest 19. _____ to slow Putin down. And sending tons of 20. _____ to support Ukraine.

DISCUSSION

Read the following questions and share your answers in class.

Discussion Question 1

Certain regions in Spain, such as Catalonia and the Basque Country, possess unique cultural, linguistic, and historical identities. They have long sought increased autonomy, or outright independence, from the central government.

If regions within the same country desire independence, do you believe it is right to pursue it? What is your opinion, and why do you think so?

Discussion Question 2

The West sought to ally with Ukraine to counter Russia, whereas Russia aimed to maintain Ukraine as a buffer zone against Western influence. Ukraine's pursuit of NATO membership resulted in a devastating war, causing significant civilian casualties and widespread destruction.

What did Ukraine gain from this conflict? Would it have been more beneficial for Ukraine to remain neutral, refrain from joining NATO, and instead seek membership in the EU to balance relations with both powers? What do you think? Why do you think so?

Unit | 2

Watch the part of the video and choose the correct answers.

01 When was the North Atlantic Treaty Organization, NATO, formed?
A 1917 B 1949 C 1991

02 How many different countries become after the collapse of the Soviet Union?
A 12 B 15 C 18

03 Which nation was aspired to join NATO alongside Ukraine?
A Georgia B Estonia C Bulgaria

04 What were the two alliance groups fighting in Europe at the beginning of the Cold War?
A NATO vs. Warsaw Pact B UN vs. Soviet C NAFTA vs. EC

05 What did happen when Ukraine signed the EU association agreement in 2013?
A signed the agreement and joined the EU
B refused to sign and strengthened ties with Russia
C signed the agreement but faced opposition from Russia

06 How long did Putin hold the Crimean Peninsula before the war?
A 5 years B 8 years C 10 years

07 When did Russia invade Ukraine territory?
A February 21st B February 24th C February 28th

08 What was the reaction from world leaders?
A surprised B unhappy C indifferent

09 How did the rest of the world help Ukraine? (Choose all that apply)
A sending military aid B opening their border to accept the refugees
C imposing economic sanctions

10 Why does the world tread carefully?
A to buy time by sacrificing Ukraine B threatened with nuclear weapons
C due to the disagreement among countries

UNIT 3 — Navigating the Trade Highway

Video title: USMCA vs NAFTA, explained with a toy car
This unit is based on the YouTube content as stated above.

Heads-up

VOCABULARY

Unit | 3

Match the vocabulary on the left with their definitions on the right.

01 take effect **A** put a plan, decision, or action into effect or to carry it out

02 tariff **B** law, rule, regulation, or agreement, becomes valid or begins to be enforced

03 immigration **C** encourage to take a particular action by offering rewards or benefits

04 source **D** a tax imposed on imported or exported goods

05 affordable **E** the dismissal of employees from their jobs

06 manufacturing **F** the action of moving to a foreign country with the intention of settling there

07 layoff **G** having the ability or inclination to compete effectively

08 implement **H** able to be bought or obtained without causing financial strain or difficulty

09 incentivize **I** to obtain something from a particular origin or supplier

10 competitive **J** the process of producing goods in large quantities

EXPRESSION

Unit | 3

Watch the video and fill in the blanks with correct expressions.

> **A** be slapped with **B** following through **C** point the finger at **D** in no way **E** in reality
> **F** by comparison **G** thanks to **H** getting out of hand **I** wouldn't know that if **J** a much of

01 0:42 ~ 0:44

And that, is _____ NAFTA.

02 1:36 ~ 1:41

Cars that didn't meet the requirement, or were made overseas, would _____ a 2.5% tariff.

03 1:47 ~ 1:54

_____, a car made in Mexico costs $1,200 less than one built in the US because labor and the parts are cheaper.

04 2:57 ~ 3:00

And Ford is _____ the only company who does this.

05 3:18 ~ 3:21

But you _____ you listened to politicians.

06 3:45 ~ 3:49

But _____, that may have less to do with NAFTA, and more to do with automation.

07 3:59 ~ 4:06

But the timing of these manufacturing layoffs, in lots of different industries, made it easy to _____ NAFTA.

08 4:14 ~ 4:18

And this opposition is why President Trump is _____ on a campaign promise.

09 4:29 ~ 4:31

But this isn't _____ a new deal.

10 5:13 ~ 5:24

What looks small on paper, when you think about the complexity and how many parts are on every car, it starts _____ fast.

FILL IN THE BLANK

Unit | 3

Watch the video and fill in the blanks with the correct words.

01 0:32 ~ 0:41
The average price of new cars has 1. _____ only 7% since the early '90s. While the price for almost all 2. _____ has increased by 86%.

02 1:04 ~ 1:18
The US, Canada and Mexico agreed to 3. _____ tariffs, which are taxes on most imported and exported goods. The countries hoped it would increase investments and that by strengthening Mexico's economy, it would slow 4. _____.

03 1:29 ~ 1:41
If at least 62.5% of a car's parts were sourced from North America, it would be 5. _____. Cars that didn't meet the requirement, or were made 6. _____, would be slapped with a 2.5% tariff.

04 3:02 ~ 3:14
About 7. _____ of the cars sold in the US meet the standards to avoid tariffs, including most cars produced by the top four auto brands. The US is actually producing more cars now than 8. _____.

05 3:45 ~ 3:49
But in reality, that may have 9. _____ with NAFTA, and 10. _____ with automation.

06 3:59 ~ 4:05
But the timing of these manufacturing 11. _____, in lots of different industries, made it easy to point the finger 12. _____.

07 4:37 ~ 4:47
Because it would require cars be made with 75% North 13. _____. And that 40-45% of those parts must be made by workers who earn at least 14. _____.

08 5:14 ~ 5:24
What looks small 15. _____, when you think about the complexity and how many parts are on every car, it starts getting 16. _____ fast.

09 5:49 ~ 6:01
But the USMCA could actually incentivize car companies to 17. _____ North America. NAFTA made US car companies more competitive with the 18. _____, and even attracted foreign car companies to build in North America.

10 6:14 ~ 6:23
So while NAFTA has kept cars pretty 19. _____ to produce, the USMCA could change that. And consumers will likely be the ones to 20. _____.

Read the following questions and share your answers in class.

Discussion Question 1

International e-commerce giants such as Temu, AliExpress, and Amazon have entered the Korean market with significant financial resources, potentially disrupting the local market ecosystem.

Should the Korean government regulate domestic market expansions, follow free trade principles, and let the market self-regulate? What do you think? Why do you think so?

Discussion Question 2

The EU removed obstacles to trade among member countries and promoted the free movement of labor, capital, services, and commodities by forming a unified market. As a result, trade among member countries has increased, strengthening their economic unification.

To protect its domestic technology industry, China has restricted the entry of foreign companies and implemented protective trade policies, including providing supportive funds for its own companies. As a result, the Chinese technology industry has grown rapidly and gained competitiveness in the global market.

What is your opinion, and why do you think so?

QUIZ

Unit | 3

Watch the part of the video and choose the correct answers.

01 How did the cost of building a new car change in 25 years?
- **A** It increased significantly.
- **B** It decreased significantly.
- **C** It did not change much.

02 How much is cheaper if you build a car in Mexico?
- **A** $500
- **B** $1,200
- **C** $1,500

03 What percentage of cars sold in the US are able to avoid tariffs under NAFTA?
- **A** Approximately 25%
- **B** Approximately 50%
- **C** Approximately 75%

04 What does NAFTA do in international trade between members?
- **A** eliminate tariffs
- **B** provide financial aid
- **C** Become a big economic community like the EU

05 How much tax applies if 70% of car parts are from North America under NAFTA?
- **A** 0% (No tariff)
- **B** 2.5%
- **C** 5%

06 Why did the large layoff happen, according to the video?
- **A** NAFTA
- **B** automation
- **C** USMCA

07 What accounts for fewer than 5% of US job losses from layoffs?
- **A** automation and technological advancements
- **B** trade with Mexico and other international agreements
- **C** outsourcing of jobs to countries like China

08 Why did President Trump claim USMCA replaced NAFTA?
- **A** It eliminated all tariffs on cars.
- **B** It increased the percentage of North American-sourced parts.
- **C** It reduced car prices significantly.

09 Is USMCA re-branding of NAFTA?
- **A** Yes, it is.
- **B** No, it is not.
- **C** Those two are totally different deal.

10 What challenges will companies face with USMCA implementation?
- **A** lose competitiveness in the global market
- **B** able to produce more goods in the US
- **C** No change from NAFTA

18 | HiEnglish

UNIT 4 — Breaking Phone Addiction

Video title: It's not you. Phones are designed to be addicting.
This unit is based on the YouTube content as stated above.

Heads-up

VOCABULARY

Unit | 4

Match the vocabulary on the left with their definitions on the right.

01 addiction
A to counteract or cancel the effect or influence of something

02 coordinate
B a strong and harmful need to regularly have or do something

03 notification
C a message or signal that provides information or updates about something

04 simulate
D a mass of whirling fluid or air, especially a whirlpool

05 replicate
E in a sincere and authentic manner

06 gravitate
F to imitate the appearance, character, or conditions of something

07 neutralize
G to make an exact copy of something

08 vortex
H an interruption or disturbance that takes focus away from something else

09 distraction
I to move toward or be attracted to something or someone

10 genuinely
J to organize the different parts of an activity or plan so that they work together effectively

EXPRESSION

Unit | 4

Watch the video and fill in the blanks with correct expressions.

> Ⓐ except for   Ⓑ in-the-moment   Ⓒ grab your attention   Ⓓ genuinely worth   Ⓔ aims to curb
> Ⓕ keep us hooked   Ⓖ grab bag of   Ⓗ built-in   Ⓘ refresh an inbox   Ⓙ rely on

01 0:11 ~ 0:14

There's a new app that _____ phone addiction.

02 1:04 ~ 1:06

It's not designed to help us, it's just designed to _____.

03 1:11 ~ 1:16

It starts with turning off all notifications, _____. when a real human is trying to reach you.

04 1:49 ~ 1:54

You could easily see emails as they came in, so you didn't have to repeatedly open your phone to _____.

05 1:58 ~ 2:03

So, every time you check it, you get this _____ notifications that can make you feel a broad variety of emotions.

06 3:44 ~ 3:51

Make sure that your home screen, when you unlock it, doesn't have anything except for the _____ tools that help you live your life.

07 3:57 ~ 4:02

None of these are apps that I can fall into and then get sucked down some _____ of stuff.

08 4:09 ~ 4:17

Unlike pagination, where users have to click to load new content on another page, infinite scrolling continuously loads new material so there's no _____ endpoint.

09 4:27 ~ 4:32

Research shows that people _____ visual cues more than internal cues to stop consuming something.

10 5:14 ~ 5:18

But it's a really deep philosophical question: what is _____ your attention?

FILL IN THE BLANK

Unit | 4

Watch the video and fill in the blanks with the correct words.

01 0:18 ~ 0:30

The problem is, our devices are designed to keep us 1. _____. They're intentionally addicting. But if you understand the 2. _____ that grab your attention, you can learn to have a healthier relationship with your phone.

02 1:16 ~ 1:28

When you get a call, a text, or a message, it's usually because another person wants to communicate with you, but a lot of today's apps simulate the feeling of that kind of 3. _____, to get you to spend more time on their 4. _____.

03 2:26 ~ 2:32

Some apps even 5. _____ the process of pulling a slot machine lever with the "pull to refresh" feature. That's 6. _____ design choice.

04 2:44 ~ 2:50

Research shows that 7. _____ notifications, where phones deliver a batch of updates at set times, reduces user 8. _____.

05 2:50 ~ 2:58

Then, you have to 9. _____ your screen. The easiest way to attract your eye's attention on a screen is through color. Human eyes are 10. _____ to warm colors.

06 3:03 ~ 3:09

That's why so many apps have 11. _____ their icons to be brighter, bolder, and warmer over the years. It's also why notification 12. _____ are red.

07 3:15 ~ 3:26

But you can neutralize that 13. _____ effect by selecting a greyscale color in your phone's accessibility settings. When you make everything black and white, your brain isn't 14. _____ thinking that this is any more important to you than this.

08 3:40 ~ 3:51

Finally, restrict your 15. _____ to everyday tools. Make sure that your home screen, when you unlock it, doesn't have anything except for the in-the-moment 16. _____ that help you live your life.

09 4:03 ~ 4:17

If you're not sure what counts as a bottomless vortex of stuff, it helps to filter out apps that use 17. _____ scrolling. Unlike pagination, where users have to click to 18. _____ new content on another page, infinite scrolling continuously loads new material so there's no built-in endpoint.

10 5:14 ~ 5:18

But it's a really deep 19. _____ question: what is 20. _____ your attention?

Read the following questions and share your answers in class.

Discussion Question 1

Given that even adults are prone to smartphone addiction, it could be more challenging for younger users to manage it. Young children often need smartphones to access school-related information. Meanwhile, Florida's governor signed a new law restricting children's social media access by prohibiting them from creating accounts.

What would be the appropriate age for children to start using smartphones? Why do you think so?

Discussion Question 2

Digital detox, a blend of 'digital' and 'detox,' is a practice that aims to rejuvenate the mind and body by breaking free from electronics, the internet, and social media. Yet, in reality, it's challenging to disconnect while working or even on weekends completely.

Should we stay engaged with digital content to maximize productivity and connectivity or be free from digital interactions to aim for mental and physical rejuvenation? What do you think? Why do you think so?

Unit | 4

Watch the part of the video and choose the correct answers.

01 What kind of problems do the 2.5 billion smartphone users experience?
- A difficulty in using the smartphone
- B difficulty in putting their phones down
- C lack of internet access

02 What did Tristan Harris explain in the video?
- A how to develop new apps
- B the history of smartphones
- C how tech companies profit off users' attention

03 How do apps simulate social interaction to keep users engaged?
- A by sending push notifications that mimic social interactions
- B by providing free content
- C by offering discounts

04 In 2003, how did push Blackberries' notifications aim to reduce phone usage?
- A by blocking irrelevant notifications
- B by extending battery life
- C by allowing users to see emails as they came in

05 How have notifications changed over time?
- A brighter to capture attention
- B match app themes
- C more muted to save battery

06 Why are slot machines mentioned in relation to phone addiction?
- A unpredictability increases addictiveness
- B visual similarity to smartphones
- C better user interfaces

07 What is the color of the notification bubble?
- A color that matches the new design and theme
- B brighter red to grab attention
- C black-and-white colors to lessen the distortion

08 What is the reason behind restricting the home screen?
- A to improve phone performance
- B to minimize distractions
- C to make the phone look organized

09 What aspect did the introduction of the self-refilling bowl illustrate?
- A Continuously providing content, making it harder for users to stop
- B A system that offers rewards for continued use
- C A method to improve user satisfaction

10 Why is infinite scrolling considered more addictive than pagination?
- A It creates a frictionless experience with no built-in endpoint.
- B It is visually more appealing.
- C It requires less data usage.

UNIT 5 The Hidden Dangers of Sliding Sports

Video title: The hidden reason Olympic sledding is so dangerous
This unit is based on the YouTube content as stated above.

Heads-up

VOCABULARY

Unit | 5

Match the vocabulary on the left with their definitions on the right.

01 inevitability — **A** causing or relating to physical or emotional injury or shock

02 traumatic — **B** the quality of being certain to happen

03 diagnosed — **C** the state of being subjected to something, especially something harmful or unpleasant

04 concussions — **D** identified or recognized as a particular disease or condition through examination or analysis

05 inherently — **E** in a permanent, essential, or characteristic way

06 g-force — **F** temporary unconsciousness or confusion caused by a blow to the head

07 exposure — **G** required by law or rules

08 neurological — **H** the force exerted on a body as a result of acceleration or gravity

09 correlates — **I** items or phenomena that are closely related or connected in some way

10 mandatory — **J** relating to the study or disorders of the nervous system

EXPRESSION

Unit | 5

Watch the video and fill in the blanks with correct expressions.

> Ⓐ in a way Ⓑ FDA-approved Ⓒ tossed about Ⓓ blown your nose Ⓔ like a snowball
> Ⓕ stroll-on Ⓖ in a given period Ⓗ a-ha moment Ⓘ flagged for Ⓙ dust yourself off

01 2:37 ~ 2:44

And essentially if you have the will and the desire to get back up and _____. and do it again, so be it.

02 3:21 ~ 3:24

Sledding is, _____, inherently brain rattling.

03 3:25 ~ 3:27

Even during the smoothest ride, a sledder is _____.

04 3:31 ~ 3:40

It's so extreme that if you haven't gone to the bathroom if you haven't _____ and if you haven't stretched you have no idea what's going to happen to you.

05 4:09 ~ 4:12

Going for a _____ earth, you're experiencing 1 g-force.

06 5:04 ~ 5:09

There are even international guidelines about how much vibration someone should encounter _____.

07 5:59 ~ 6:06

I get out and I haven't had a crash or nothing would happen but that just built up over time _____.

08 6:38 ~ 6:41

It was like a _____ for me.

09 7:21 ~ 7:30

A simple sensor system could detect an impact and have that per person immediately _____ treatment and possibly sitting out until they've recovered fully.

10 7:38 ~ 7:43

Or an _____ collar that increases blood volume in your brain giving it better cushioning.

FILL IN THE BLANK

Unit | 5

Watch the video and fill in the blanks with the correct words.

01 0:00 ~ 0:06
In bobsleigh, luge and skeleton, collectively known as 1. _____ crashes are an 2. _____ .

02 0:36 ~ 0:45
But in the years after she 3. _____ , she started to experience 4. _____ . Long-term, short-term memory loss, anxiety, fear, depression.

03 1:21 ~ 1:40
There's growing evidence that, when it comes to the sliding sports catastrophic concussions like the ones you get from crashing might not be the 5. _____ of brain injury. Microconcussions are. Concussions so mild they can often go unnoticed and so common that they have a special name: 6. _____ .

04 3:00 ~ 3:06
So a lot of those 7. _____ . It's all those little things that 8. _____ sled head.

05 3:10 ~ 3:24
From the outside, sledding sports 9. _____ . A graceful, if fast, run down an icy track. But, inside a sled, things look and feel very different. Sledding is, in a way, inherently 10. _____ .

06 4:25 ~ 4:46
The g-force of an 11. _____ is hard to measure or generalize but one researcher found that most diagnosed ones have a g-force between 85 and 95. And, when another researcher measured the g-force of his own skeleton ride at the Whistler Olympic track 12. _____ , here, he recorded 84.5 g-force.

07 4:56 ~ 5:09
Long term exposure to 13. _____ can lead to a range of serious health issues affecting basically all of your body's systems. There are even international guidelines about how much vibration someone should 14. _____ in a given period.

08 6:27 ~ 6:37
When doctors analyzed her results, they saw this: roughly, the red shading correlates to 15. _____ . In a brain that hadn't experienced 16. _____ those areas would be white.

09 7:17 ~ 7:30
One way to better 17. _____ sliding athletes is to require them to wear a monitor. A simple sensor system could detect an impact and have that 18. _____ immediately flagged for treatment and possibly sitting out until they've recovered fully.

10 7:59 ~ 8:08
It depends on international 19. _____ to make these 20. _____ changes and start looking at their athletes as actually things that keep the body alive.

DISCUSSION

Read the following questions and share your answers in class.

Discussion Question 1

In boxing, when safety problems such as injuries, lethargy, and death occurred during matches, amateur games made it mandatory to wear helmets. To reduce safety issues for players, they increased the weight of the gloves. As a result of the disappearance of power and technology-oriented games, boxing has lost its true fun, and instead, careful games centered on scoring points have become the norm. Therefore, there is a trend towards a return to traditional practices, such as not wearing a helmet and reducing the weight of gloves.

Does the safety of players come first, or does the fun of sports come first? What is your opinion? Why do you think so?

Discussion Question 2

Some believe extreme sports such as triathlons, the 7 Summits Challenge, and ultra-marathons provide an exhilarating adrenaline rush and foster a deep passion for these activities. They argue that these sports embody the spirit of challenging the impossible, affirming human willpower, and advancing technology and materials to benefit our physical and mental health.

However, others argue that we must distinguish between adventurous and reckless challenges. Sports like wingsuit flying, building climbing, freediving, and the Isle of Man TT are considered extremely dangerous, with a high risk of fatal accidents. They believe such activities are excessively hazardous and advocate for safety restrictions or even banning them altogether.

Do the advantages of extreme sports outweigh the risks, or should we restrict or outlaw certain dangerous activities? What do you think? Why do you think so?

Unit | 5

Watch the part of the video and choose the correct answers.

01 Why are crashes inevitable in bobsleigh, luge, and skeleton?
- A poorly maintained tracks
- B the speed and nature of the sports
- C equipment failure

02 What symptoms did Christina Smith experience after retiring from bobsledding?
- A joint pain and muscle stiffness
- B vision impairment and hearing loss
- C long-term memory loss and emotional regulation issues

03 How does sledding have different effects on the brain than other sports?
- A causes more nerve cell damage
- B Less severe despite high speeds
- C disperses impact across the body

04 What analogy describes the sledding experience about vibrations and g-forces?
- A swimming in turbulent waters
- B walking on a bumpy road
- C riding a roller coaster

05 What is the brain's chain reaction that occurs after microconcussions?
- A They release toxins that harm other neurons.
- B They trigger immediate unconsciousness.
- C They lead to rapid healing of brain tissue.

06 Why is exposure to high g-forces for milliseconds a concern?
- A massive impact in a short time
- B trigger immediate unconsciousness
- C lead to rapid brain healing

07 What could Christina discern from the qEEG results?
- A Vigorous brain activity
- B Athletes experience it repeatedly
- C G-forces are paired with impact

08 Why does the video suggest using sensors in sliding sports?
- A to monitor athletes' speed during races
- B for better performance
- C to detect impacts for medical attention

09 What is one of the proposed solutions to improve athlete safety in sliding sports?
- A shortening the sliding tracks
- B requiring athletes to wear additional protective gear
- C reduce the number of competitive events

10 What role do international bodies play in improving athlete safety?
- A They are not related at all.
- B They provide funding for technological advancements.
- C They have the authority to enforce safety regulations.

UNIT 6 — Inequality and Climate Change

Video title: How America's hottest city is trying to cool down
This unit is based on the YouTube content as stated above.

Heads-up

VOCABULARY

Unit | 6

Match the vocabulary on the left with their definitions on the right.

01 inequality

A the hard surface of streets and sidewalks

02 poverty

B ability to reflect sunlight rather than absorb it

03 vulnerable

C being susceptible to harm or adverse impacts

04 pavement

D the state of being extremely poor or lacking sufficient financial resources

05 capture

E disparity or difference in conditions, resources, or opportunities

06 mitigate

F trim or cut back parts of plants to improve their health, appearance, or productivity

07 reflective

G the process of dividing a market into distinct groups based on characteristics

08 carbon footprint

H the balance or exchange between different factors or options

09 tradeoff

I lessen the severity or impact of something

10 prune

J traps and retains heat, exacerbating local temperatures

EXPRESSION

Unit | 6

Watch the video and fill in the blanks with correct expressions.

> Ⓐ grappling with Ⓑ water bill Ⓒ fall on Ⓓ a family of four Ⓔ Phoenix native
> Ⓕ little pocket Ⓖ beams into Ⓗ shade shelter Ⓘ the forecasted high Ⓙ their choice

01 0:36 ~ 0:38

An excessive heat warning is _____.

02 0:41 ~ 0:44

The city's _____ an increase in heat related deaths.

03 0:58 ~ 1:01

_____ that day was 112 degrees Fahrenheit.

04 1:23 ~ 1:25

She's a local community advocate and _____.

05 1:38 ~ 1:41

The average income level for _____ is about $19,000.

06 2:06 ~ 2:07

So we're like a _____.

07 2:52 ~ 2:53

The sun just _____ all that pavement.

08 5:30 ~ 5:34

Because there's that tradeoff between shade or increased _____.

09 6:07 ~ 6:14

But she also hoped for some more basic things: like sidewalks, and _____ for all the bus stops.

10 6:22 ~ 6:32

And that's what will have to change if cities like Phoenix want to make sure that the heaviest burdens of climate warming don't _____ those who are least prepared to withstand them.

FILL IN THE BLANK

Unit | 6

Watch the video and fill in the blanks with the correct words.

01 0:21 ~ 0:28
The 1. _____ is pretty obvious. This is where it becomes clear that climate change and wealth inequality are not really 2. _____ issues.

02 0:49 ~ 0:54
" 3. _____ is one factor causing rising temperature. 4. _____ is the other."

03 1:09 ~ 1:18
So here I am in a neighborhood with some of the 5. _____ surface temperatures, but when I drove 8 miles north of there, I was in one of the 6. _____ parts of Phoenix.

04 2:26 ~ 2:33
This is the Sonoran Desert, so 7. _____ the summers are hot. But it also seems like this entire city was almost 8. _____ capture heat.

05 3:15 ~ 3:24
The thermal image shows the 9. _____ of the dark roof is hotter than the white ones. And the city has also tried painting some roads with a more reflective 10. _____.

06 3:41 ~ 3:47
And studies have confirmed that the 11. _____ of cool roofs and cool pavements is smaller than the cooling effect of 12. _____.

07 4:27 ~ 4:35
So the city of Phoenix has committed funds to 13. _____ more trees. They want all neighborhoods to reach a minimal level of 14. _____ by 2030.

08 4:44 ~ 4:53
Outside of parks and along major streets, the 15. _____ currently depends not on public resources, but on 16. _____ ones.

09 5:35 ~ 5:40
But it's the cost of 17. _____ the trees that is challenging, obviously in a 18. _____ neighborhood like ours.

10 6:22 ~ 6:29
And that's what will have to change if cities like Phoenix want to make sure that the 19. _____ of climate warming don't fall on those who are least prepared to 20. _____ them.

Read the following questions and share your answers in class.

Discussion Question 1

The management of extreme heat exhibits a stark contrast. While higher-income individuals can use their resources to tackle heat-related challenges, low-income neighborhoods often struggle due to inadequate infrastructure and a lack of greenery.

What should governments do to mitigate the effects of extreme heat on low-income communities? What is your opinion? Why do you think so?

Discussion Question 2

Some argue that the benefits of developing natural resources primarily go to a few wealthy individuals. They suggest that the government should tax the rich and use the funds to help the poor mitigate the impacts of climate change as a solution.

Others believe that fossil fuel development and carbon emissions have significantly contributed to climate change and that electric vehicles and solar energy are viable alternatives. Therefore, they advocate for substantial investment in developing alternative energy sources for the future.

What is your perspective on this issue, and why? Please share your thoughts with us.

Unit | 6

Watch the part of the video and choose the correct answers.

01 What does the script suggest about the relationship between heat and poverty?
- A Higher poverty areas have higher temperatures.
- B Poverty decreases with higher temperatures.
- C No correlation between them.

02 What makes neighborhoods like Central City South vulnerable to heat?
- A proximity to parks and green spaces
- B access to air-conditioned public spaces only
- C wide streets and lack of shade

03 How does urban development in Phoenix contribute to heat retention?
- A increasing community engagement
- B reducing parking lots
- C using reflective coatings on roads and roofs

04 Which urban design elements in Phoenix increase heat, according to the video?
- A rooftop gardens and green roofs
- B lack of greenery
- C narrow streets and dense building clusters

05 When comparing reflective coating and trees, which is better for cooling?
- A Reflective coating is better.
- B Trees is more effective.
- C Both are equally effective.

06 Why does the video argue that initiatives like reflective coating are insufficient?
- A Reflective surfaces are costly to maintain.
- B Trees don't sequester carbon.
- C Trees offer more benefits like shade and biodiversity.

07 Why is it challenging to maintaining greenery in low-income neighborhoods?
- A lack of community interest
- B high tree planting rates
- C limited funding and resources for tree maintenance

08 What initiatives has Phoenix took to deal with heat resilience?
- A committed funds for tree planting
- B subsidized private tree maintenance
- C implemented water conservation measures

09 How does wealth inequality impact access to essential infrastructure in Phoenix?
- A Low-income areas lack sidewalks and shade.
- B Wealthy areas are more heat vulnerable.
- C Wealthy areas lack public transportation.

10 How can Phoenix achieve equitable urban planning and climate resilience?
- A subsidizing private tree planting
- B private-funded tree initiatives
- C investing in shade shelters and better sidewalks

36 | HiEnglish

UNIT 7 — Artificial Intelligence in Warfare

Video title: How AI tells Israel who to bomb
This unit is based on the YouTube content as stated above.

Heads-up

VOCABULARY

Unit | 7

Match the vocabulary on the left with their definitions on the right.

01	artificial intelligence	**A** the use of technology to perform tasks without human intervention
02	respects	**B** particular aspects, points, or details
03	swiftness	**C** allowed or permitted by rules, laws, or other authoritative standards
04	accuracy	**D** unintended damage, injuries, or deaths caused to civilians or their property
05	surveillance	**E** the quality or state of being correct or precise
06	collateral damage	**F** close observation of a suspected spy or criminal
07	permissible	**G** technology that enables machines to simulate human intelligence
08	validity	**H** non-military individuals who are injured or killed during conflicts or military operations
09	civilian casualties	**I** the quality of being logically or factually sound
10	automation	**J** the quality of being fast or quick

EXPRESSION

Unit | 7

Watch the video and fill in the blanks with correct expressions.

> **A** and etc. **B** on the contrary **C** compared to **D** aches my heart **E** hone in
> **F** matched against **G** supposedly **H** in shock **I** in conjunction with **J** in a strange way

01 0:30 ~ 0:33
We received a picture of our house and we were _____.

02 1:10 ~ 1:20
But after over 34,000 Palestinians killed, _____ just over 1,400 in Israel's 2014 war in Gaza, it's clear something different is happening.

03 2:09 ~ 2:17
And what it does is it uses advanced image-processing algorithms to _____ on a target, sort of like a an auto-aim in Call of Duty.

04 2:30 ~ 2:34
Their facial images and other biometrics are being _____ a database.

05 2:54 ~ 2:57
It does this by working _____ other AI tools.

06 4:07 ~ 4:17
The Gospel creates an output which suggests specific possible targets, possible munitions, warnings of possible collateral damage, _____.

07 5:12 ~ 5:21
But even when determining the 90% of _____ correct targets, Israel also expanded the definition of a Hamas operative for the first time.

08 6:01 ~ 6:14
So _____, the less of a danger you posed, then they used less sophisticated bombs, therefore maybe creating more collateral damage.

09 8:38 ~ 8:50
And _____, I think a lot of the momentum of these technological initiatives needs to be interrupted, in whatever ways we can.

10 8:51 ~ 8:55
It really _____ that these moments are never going to be back.

FILL IN THE BLANK

Unit | 7

Watch the video and fill in the blanks with the correct words.

01 0:40 ~ 0:55
Heba didn't know exactly why her home had been 1. _____. But over the past few months, Israeli journalists have found that much of the destruction in Gaza since the attacks of October 7th has been enabled and often 2. _____ an artificial intelligence system.

02 1:04 ~ 1:20
The whole dream of AI is that it would offer these 3. _____. But after over 34,000 Palestinians killed, compared to just over 1,400 in Israel's 2014 war in Gaza, it's clear 4. _____ is happening.

03 2:35 ~ 2:45
But we're now learning more about the 5. _____ that choose 6. _____ in Gaza, from two reports in the Israeli publications +972 and Local Call.

04 2:49 ~ 2:58
Gospel is a system that 7. _____ bombing targets for specific buildings and structures in Gaza. It does this by working in 8. _____ with other AI tools.

05 4:30 ~ 4:44
Multiple sources who spoke to +972 reported that the idea behind power targets is to exert 9. _____ on Hamas. Heba's home was most likely one of the 10. _____ picked up by the Gospel system.

06 4:57 ~ 5:11
As the Israel-Hamas war began, Lavender used historic data and surveillance to 11. _____ as many as 37,000 Hamas and Islamic Jihad targets. Sources told +972 that about 10% of those targets are 12. _____.

07 6:15 ~ 6:29
Sources told reporters that for every junior Hamas operative that Lavender marked, operative that Lavender marked, it was permissible to kill up to 15 or 20 13. _____. But also that for some targets, the number of permissible civilian casualties was 14. _____ 300.

08 6:38 ~ 6:44
AI systems do not produce 15. _____. They only produce 16. _____, just like a weather forecast or the stock market.

09 7:11 ~ 7:17
Which brings us to the 17. _____ of both of these processes: 18. _____.

10 7:40 ~ 7:48
Experts have been telling us that essentially what's happening in Gaza is an 19. _____ site for 20. _____ AI technologies.

Unit | 7

Read the following questions and share your answers in class.

Discussion Question 1

AI can process data faster and more accurately than humans and perform dangerous tasks on our behalf. However, AI can also eliminate standardized jobs such as legal work, accounting, and translation and contribute to cyber crimes like deepfakes.

How should we accept and use AI? What is your opinion? Why do you think so?

Discussion Question 2

Using AI technology, Israel has significantly improved military efficiency and protected its citizens. The 'Iron Dome' uses AI algorithms to quickly identify threats and calculate interception trajectories, effectively blocking attacks with high accuracy and protecting the lives of its citizens.

On the other hand, the Israeli Defense Forces (IDF) have faced criticism for using AI systems to select bombing targets in Gaza, where predictions by AI and human reviews were not adequately conducted, resulting in many civilian casualties.

The use of AI in military applications raises ethical issues. How should we approach and address these problems? What are your thoughts on this? Why do you think so?

Unit | 7

Watch the part of the video and choose the correct answers.

01 Why is the death toll of 34,000 Palestinians significant?
  A It represents casualties from a single attack.   B It suggests issues with AI targeting.
  C It is the highest death toll in recent conflicts.

02 What does the IDF's use of AI systems like Iron Dome and SMASH illustrate?
  A It coordinates defensive strategies.   B It identifies and categorizes bombing targets.
  C It provides training for soldiers.

03 What is the role of the Gospel system in the IDF's operations?
  A It coordinates defensive strategies.   B It identifies and categorizes bombing targets.
  C It provides training for soldiers.

04 How do Fire Factory's target categories reflect the IDF's strategy?
  A avoids residential areas   B prioritizes underground tunnels
  C mixes military and civilian targets

05 What does the concept of "power targets" reveal about the IDF's strategy?
  A It focuses on destroying military hardware.   B It seeks to minimize civilian casualties.
  C It aims to pressure Hamas by targeting civilian infrastructure.

06 What is the Lavender system's primary function in the IDF's military strategy?
  A to collect surveillance data from checkpoints   B to target specific individuals
  C to produce bombing targets for buildings

07 Why does the video highlight the need for human approval ?
  A AI operates without errors.   B Human approval slows the process.
  C Human judgment is vital.

08 How did the definition of a Hamas operative change with the Lavender system?
  A more specific to military personnel   B focused on high-ranking officials
  C excluded civil society members

09 Does AI provide factual information, according to the video?
  A Yes, it provides concrete facts.   B No, it only produces predictions.
  C Yes, it verifies details through human analysis.

10 What are the consequences of using AI in warfare, as discussed in the video?
  A increased global peace and security   B enhanced precision and reduced casualties
  C greater civilian casualties

42 | HiEnglish

UNIT 8 — Impacts of Light on Sleep Cycles

Video title: How screens actually affect your sleep
This unit is based on the YouTube content as stated above.

Heads-up

VOCABULARY

Unit | 8

Match the vocabulary on the left with their definitions on the right.

01 malleable — **A** a unit of absolute temperature and a base unit of thermodynamic temperature

02 melatonin — **B** easily influenced or altered

03 suppress — **C** to fill something to the point where no more can be held or absorbed

04 Kelvin (K) — **D** relating to the natural processes that occur in a 24-hour cycle

05 spectrum — **E** a hormone regulates sleep and wakefulness

06 counteract — **F** to control or influence a person or situation skillfully

07 manipulate — **G** to prevent the development, action, or expression of something

08 circadian — **H** to act against something in order to reduce its force or neutralize it

09 saturate — **I** a range of different things, usually colors or light waves

10 disruption — **J** a significant interruption that alters the normal flow or functioning of a system or process

EXPRESSION

Unit | 8

Watch the video and fill in the blanks with correct expressions.

> **A** the beauty of **B** lack thereof **C** aka **D** not just, any other **E** touched on
> **F** kick start **G** might be wondering **H** catch up **I** wrecking **J** can't resist

01 0:11 ~ 0:12

Even sleep experts _____.

02 0:15 ~ 0:20

Yes, just to _____ on my calendar and email, it's always less than 30 minutes for me.

03 0:26 ~ 0:35

As a chronic screen's before bed guy myself, I went into our conversation wanting to know if there is any way that we could keep using our phones at night without completely _____ our sleep schedules.

04 0:46 ~ 0:54

Before we dive into the science, let's first get a quick review on how our body responds to natural light like the sun. and the _____.

05 1:03 ~ 1:08

Melatonin is _____ hormone. It's kind of an internal timekeeper.

06 1:30 ~ 1:37

This natural color shift, combined with the decreasing brightness, tells our body to _____ the production of melatonin, which makes us feel sleepy.

07 2:04 ~ 2:11

The phone's artificial daylight, _____ blue light, suppresses the production of melatonin, disrupting our feelings of sleepiness.

08 2:12 ~ 2:17

Now, You _____, don't phones have a built in feature that's intended to counteract this blue light?

09 4:52 ~ 4:57

So that's _____ your circadian system. You can use its own mechanisms against it.

10 5:18 ~ 5:20

And we haven't even _____ them all yet.

FILL IN THE BLANK

Unit | 8

Watch the video and fill in the blanks with the correct words.

01 0:00 ~ 0:08

If you've heard anything about sleep science, it's probably that you're 1. _____ use any screens before bed. And if you're anything like me, you've probably 2. _____ that advice.

02 0:58 ~ 1:08

This is because your body produces 3. _____, a hormone that plays a huge role in sleep. melatonin is not just, any other hormone. It's kind of an internal 4. _____.

03 1:09 ~ 1:15

As the sun rises and you get exposed to its 5. _____, your body suppresses the production of melatonin, helping you feel 6. _____.

04 1:30 ~ 1:37

This natural color 7. _____, combined with the decreasing brightness, tells our body to kick start the production of melatonin, which makes us feel 8. _____.

05 2:04 ~ 2:11

The phone's artificial daylight, aka 9. _____, suppresses the production of melatonin, 10. _____ our feelings of sleepiness.

06 2:29 ~ 2:37

It's a very smart feature, The idea is right, they're trying to 11. _____ a lighting characteristic, which is the 12. _____, to reduce the circadian effectiveness.

07 2:57 ~ 3:07

And while that makes it sound like Night Shift doesn't work, it's actually a lot more 13. _____ than that. Spectrum is just one 14. _____. Distribution duration, timing and amount need to be considered.

08 4:10 ~ 4:15

So we know that limiting screen 15. _____, shifting the colors warmer, and lowering the 16. _____ all helps.

09 4:52 ~ 5:03

So that's the beauty of your 17. _____ system. You can use its own mechanisms against it. So basically, if you go for a sunny walk in the morning, you could potentially 18. _____ the amount of circadian disruption.

10 5:06 ~ 5:17

At the end of the day, body 19. _____ aside, the thing that I realized as I was researching this story is that there are so many more 20. _____ that impact our sleep besides just the blue light that comes out of ourphones.

DISCUSSION

Read the following questions and share your answers in class.

Discussion Question 1

In Western cultures, a proverb states, 'Sleep is better than medicine.' This underscores the importance of sleep for well-being. However, in contemporary society, the widespread adoption of smartphones has led many people to face sleep-related issues, such as insomnia.

Individuals should take control and manage their smartphone usage effectively before bedtime to enhance sleep quality. What is your idea, and tell us why?

Discussion Question 2

Artificial light adversely affects humans by disrupting our behaviors, such as sleep and birth. Meanwhile, artificial lighting ensures human safety and supports economic activities.

Does the benefit of artificial lighting outweigh its controversy? What do you think? Why do you think so?

Unit | 8

Watch the part of the video and choose the correct answers.

01 Why are screens typically discouraged before bedtime?
  Ⓐ They emit harmful radiation.   Ⓑ They disrupt the production of melatonin.
  Ⓒ They interfere with REM sleep.

02 How does natural sunlight influence the body's production of melatonin?
  Ⓐ It stimulates melatonin production.   Ⓑ It suppresses melatonin production.
  Ⓒ It decreases melatonin sensitivity.

03 How does the natural light shifts regulate sleep?
  Ⓐ They signal the body to increase cortisol levels.   Ⓑ They reduce serotonin production.
  Ⓒ They prompt melatonin release for sleep preparation.

04 Why is melatonin suppression by blue light relevant to sleep quality?
  Ⓐ It delays sleep onset.   Ⓑ It shortens REM sleep cycles.
  Ⓒ It affects memory consolidation during sleep.

05 If the color temperature is 4,500 K, what would your brain do?
  Ⓐ start producing melatonin   Ⓑ stay awake and alert
  Ⓒ no action caused by the color temperature

06 How effective is Night Shift in reducing sleep disruption?
  Ⓐ eliminates blue light impact   Ⓑ no noticeable effect
  Ⓒ reduces sleep disruption

07 What are the long-term consequences of screen time before bed?
  Ⓐ increased risk of cardiovascular disease   Ⓑ decreased melatonin sensitivity
  Ⓒ enhanced cognitive function

08 What was the strategy to counteract the effects of evening screen use on sleep?
  Ⓐ increasing morning light exposure   Ⓑ decreasing exposure to natural light
  Ⓒ avoiding screens altogether

09 What is circadian disruption according to the video?
  Ⓐ natural alignment of your body clock   Ⓑ adjusting sleep schedule for work or travel
  Ⓒ disturbance of your body clock by artificial light

10 What advice improves sleep quality when using a device?
  Ⓐ use in a bright room   Ⓑ avoid screens two hours before bed
  Ⓒ set a consistent screen schedule

UNIT 9 — The Secret Behind the Shaky Inflation

Video title: Why can't prices just stay the same?
This unit is based on the YouTube content as stated above.

Heads-up

VOCABULARY

Unit | 9

Match the vocabulary on the left with their definitions on the right.

01 inflation
A the central banking system of the United States, which regulates monetary policy

02 inflation target
B a beneficial cycle that reinforces itself through a positive feedback loop

03 arbitrary
C the rate at which the general level of prices for goods and services is rising

04 virtuous cycle
D the amount charged by lenders to borrowers for the use of money

05 vicious cycle
E a specific rate of inflation that a central bank aims to achieve over a set period

06 Federal Reserve (Fed)
F a decrease in the general price level of goods and services

07 interest rate
G based on random choice or personal whim, rather than any reason or system

08 deflation
H to enhance or boost to a very high degree

09 supercharge
I a harmful cycle that reinforces itself through a negative feedback loop

10 deflation spiral
J a downward cycle where falling prices lead to reduced consumer spending and investment

EXPRESSION

Unit | 9

Watch the video and fill in the blanks with correct expressions.

> A hold off B tamping down C mind blowing D rock bottom E dipped below
> F in no small part G keep pace with H lagged behind I infuriatingly J stave off

01 0:28 ~ 0:33

But, _____, since this chart just shows a rate of change that doesn't mean that prices are down.

02 2:11 ~ 2:19

It's okay if prices rise so long as wages rise, too. You'll still be able to afford the same goods if your wages _____ inflation.

03 2:22 ~ 2:25

In the U.S. for two years, wage growth _____ inflation.

04 2:34 ~ 2:40

And that is a good thing that also we have to remember, wages in this country are _____ and had been for way, way too long, right?

05 4:18 ~ 4:22

When the Fed uses interest rates to bring down inflation, what they're doing is _____ that demand, right.

06 4:56 ~ 5:01

When prices fall, consumers may _____ on making big purchases, hoping for even lower prices in the future.

07 5:13 ~ 5:19

Unemployed people spend less, and even the people who are employed might choose to save more to _____ financial loss.

08 5:37 ~ 5:44

The last time inflation _____ 2%, in spring of 2020, the U.S. brought interest rates all the way down to 0.05%.

09 6:19 ~ 6:24

But that's thanks _____ to the high inflation that most of the world battled over the last few years.

10 6:55 ~ 6:56

And it's just it's it's _____, right?

FILL IN THE BLANK

Unit | 9

Watch the video and fill in the blanks with the correct words.

01 0:05 ~ 0:14
In 2022, much of the world experienced a period of uncommonly 1. _____. With the U.S., U.K. and Eurozone all 2. _____ around 10%.

02 1:11 ~ 1:20
The first reason inflation can't 3. _____ is because governments and their 4. _____ don't want it to. Lots of countries actively pursue what is called an "inflation target."

03 1:21 ~ 1:33
In the U.S. right now, it's about 2%. In fact, that's the number that's used by most central banks across the world. But the truth of it is that's a pretty 5. _____. The goal is what 6. _____ consider a "virtuous cycle."

04 2:22 ~ 2:28
In the U.S. for two years, 7. _____ lagged behind inflation. That trend has 8. _____ starting in mid 2023.

05 2:51 ~ 3:04
When 9. _____ interruptions created product shortages and some companies artificially 10. _____ prices to increase their profits, which along with some other causes, effectively turn this virtuous cycle into a vicious one.

06 4:18 ~ 4:28
When the Fed uses interest rates to bring down inflation, what they're doing is tamping down that 11. _____, right. They're telling people "you can't have a job" like, "let's put you out of work." So that demand slows, that, you know, 12. _____ slows.

07 4:41 ~ 4:55
But we also have to talk about what happens when prices fall 13. _____ rise. That's called "deflation." And falling prices honestly sounds 14. _____. But they can also introduce another kind of cycle: a "deflationary spiral."

08 5:58 ~ 6:14
Historically, periods of true deflation are 15. _____, but when they do happen, it seems that fixing them requires a pretty serious shock to the economy. 16. _____ was in part a deflationary spiral. Solved only by the outbreak of World War Two, when the government supercharged spending and employment.

09 6:30 ~ 6:36
The cost of deflation is really high, and that's something that we want to 17. _____. This is where 18. _____ come in.

10 7:05 ~ 7:18
If inflation sits here, that basic shakiness is constantly 19. _____ of dropping down into the deflation zone, triggering the bad cycle. And the way to prevent that is to have it sit just a little bit 20. _____.

DISCUSSION

Read the following questions and share your answers in class.

Discussion Question 1

Both inflation and deflation affect our lives. Inflation increases living expenses and decreases savings, but it also reduces debts and increases investment profits. Deflation, on the other hand, can reduce consumption and investment while increasing unemployment. However, deflation can also lower the prices of services and commodities and increase exports.

If you choose between inflation and deflation, which would you pick, and why?

Discussion Question 2

In recent years, Germany has achieved stable economic growth due to strong labor union bargaining power and economic structural reforms by the government. Australia has also achieved stable growth thanks to low unemployment and a booming mining industry. In contrast, Turkey has faced economic difficulties due to policies that have excessively lowered interest rates and political instability. The United States has encountered similar problems due to interest rate hikes and shortages of raw materials caused by global supply chain disruptions.

After COVID-19, are you satisfied with your country's wage increases and the government's role? Please explain why or why not.

Unit | 9

Watch the part of the video and choose the correct answers.

01 Why doesn't a lower inflation rate imply that prices are falling?
- A because it measures price change, not price levels.
- B because it reflects future expectations.
- C because it adjusts for seasonal variations.

02 Why do central banks set an inflation target?
- A to control savings
- B to ensure prices remain constant
- C to maintain economic stability and prevent both high inflation and deflation

03 In terms of inflation, what is a "virtuous cycle"?
- A Prices fall, leading to contraction.
- B Rising prices boost spending and growth.
- C Prices remain constant, maintaining economic stability.

04 Why is it crucial for wages to keep pace with inflation?
- A to ensure higher profits for company.
- B to maintain workers' purchasing power
- C to reduce the cost of goods and services

05 How do governments combat rising inflation?
- A lower taxes to boost spending
- B fix the prices of essential goods
- C raise interest rates to make borrowing more expensive and reduce spending.

06 What is the critical factor that must accompany rising prices for the virtuous cycle?
- A decreasing interest rates
- B increasing wages that keep pace with inflation
- C stable government policies

07 Which could disrupt the virtuous cycle and turn it into a vicious cycle?
- A continuous wage growth exceeding inflation
- B increase in the consumers' savings
- C supply chain interruptions and artificial price increases by companies

08 Why is a deflationary spiral is harmful to the economy?
- A more consumer spending due to lower prices
- B less business revenue
- C lower real debt burden making it easier for borrowers to repay loans

09 Why can't governments respond to deflation as effectively as they can to inflation?
- A fewer tools to stimulate demand
- B requires unpopular interest rate hikes
- C needs stricter banking regulations

10 What is the typical inflation target set by the Federal Reserve?
- A 0%
- B 1%
- C 2%

UNIT 10 — The Origin of the Word 'OK'

Video title: Why we say "OK"
This unit is based on the YouTube content as stated above.

Heads-up

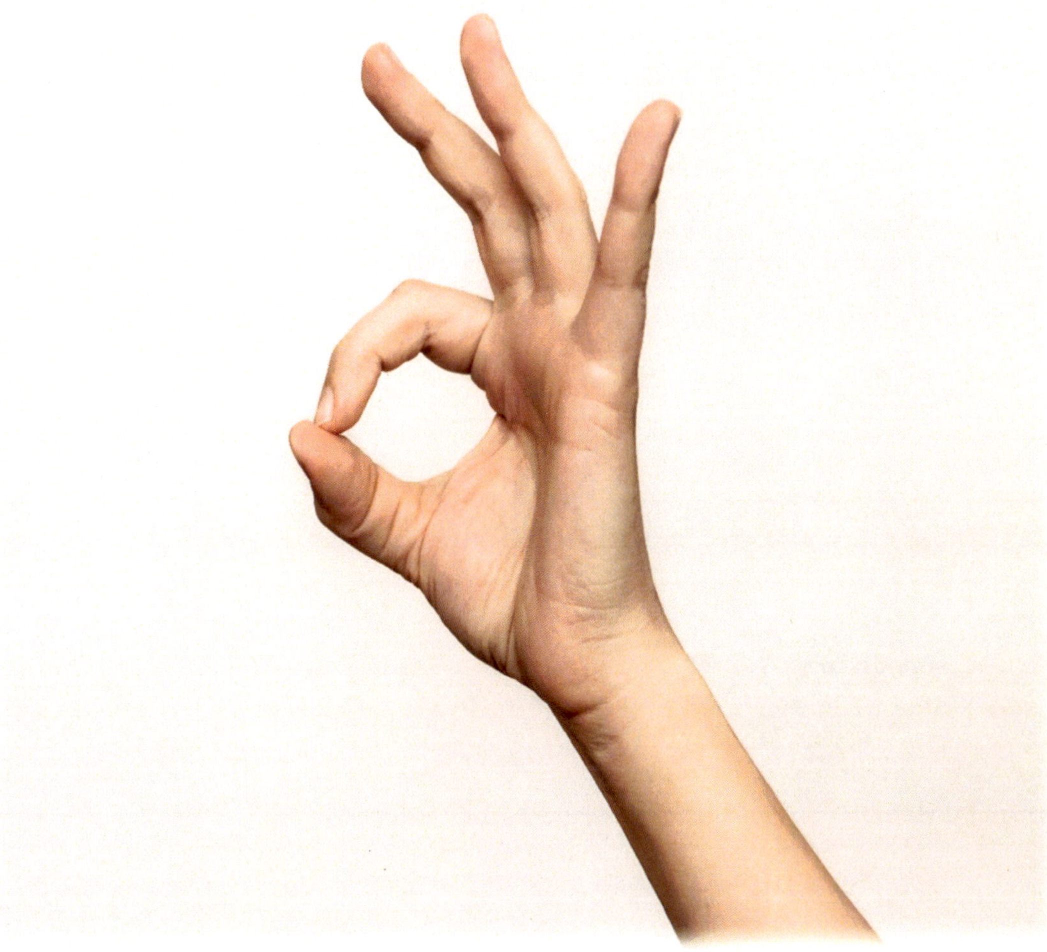

VOCABULARY

Match the vocabulary on the left with their definitions on the right.

01 intentional — **A** the language or dialect spoken by the ordinary people in a particular country or region

02 abbreviation — **B** a device for long-distance transmission of textual messages using electrical signals

03 oll korrect — **C** a shortened form of a word or phrase

04 vernacular — **D** not clearly expressed or easily understood

05 legitimate — **E** a playful misspelling of "all correct," which led to the abbreviation "OK."

06 telegraph — **F** making something continue indefinitely

07 rarity — **G** the state or quality of being rare or uncommon

08 perpetuating — **H** done on purpose

09 obscure — **I** expressing agreement or consent

10 affirmative — **J** conforming to the law or to rules

EXPRESSION

Unit | 10

Watch the video and fill in the blanks with correct expressions.

> A serious business B keep track of C stuck around D very unlikely E going mainstream
> F out of fashion G katch your eyes H settled I rose above J moment to shine

01 0:56 ~ 1:02

But thanks to a couple of lucky breaks, one abbreviation _____ the rest: OK, or "oll korrect."

02 1:09 ~ 1:17

Its abbreviated cousin started _____ on March 23, 1839, when OK was first published in the Boston Morning Post.

03 2:06 ~ 2:17

And while similar abbreviations fell _____, OK made the crossover from slang into legitimate, functional use thanks to one invention: the telegraph.

04 2:41 ~ 2:42

This was OK's _____.

05 2:43 ~ 2:46

The two letters were easy to tap out and _____ to be confused with anything else.

06 3:04 ~ 3:05

OK had become _____.

07 3:06 ~ 3:10

But there's another big reason the two letters _____, and it's not just because they're easy to communicate.

08 3:23 ~ 3:31

That rarity spurred a "Kraze for K" at the turn of the century in advertising and print, where companies replaced hard Cs with Ks in order to _____.

09 4:31 ~ 4:32

It's _____, then!

10 4:51 ~ 4:56

It's is sort of a reflex at this point — we don't even _____ how much we use it.

FILL IN THE BLANK

Unit | 10

Watch the video and fill in the blanks with the correct words.

01 0:00 ~ 0:02 & 0:11 ~ 0:13

There's a 1. _____ word that we hear everywhere.
& OK might be the most 2. _____

02 0:36 ~ 0:54

OK actually traces back to an 1830s fad of intentionally 3. _____ abbreviations. Young "intellectual" types in Boston delighted those "in the know" with 4. _____ coded messages such as KC, or "knuff ced", KY, "know yuse," and OW, "oll wright."

03 1:09 ~ 1:25

Its abbreviated cousin started going mainstream on March 23, 1839, when OK was first 5. _____ in the Boston Morning Post. Soon other papers picked up on the joke and spread it around the country, until OK was something everyone knew about, not just a few Boston 6. _____.

04 1:35 ~ 1:45

Van Buren's 7. _____ formed OK Clubs all over the country, and their message was pretty clear: Old Kinderhook was "oll korrect." The campaign was highly publicized and turned pretty nasty in the 8. _____.

05 2:01 ~ 2:17

That 1840 presidential campaign firmly established OK in the American 9. _____. And while similar abbreviations fell out of fashion, OK made the crossover from slang into legitimate, functional use thanks to one invention: the 10. _____.

06 2:41 ~ 2:46

This was OK's moment to shine. The two letters were easy to 11. _____ and very unlikely to be 12. _____ with anything else.

07 3:04 ~ 3:14

OK had become serious business. But there's another big reason the two letters stuck around, and it's not just because they're easy to 13. _____. It has to do with how OK looks. Or more specifically, how the 14. _____ looks and sounds.

08 3:23 ~ 3:39

That 15. _____ spurred a "Kraze for K" at the turn of the century in advertising and print, where companies replaced hard Cs with Ks in order to Katch your eye. The idea was that modifying a word — like Klearflax Linen Rugs or this Kook-Rite Stove, for example — would draw more 16. _____ to it.

09 4:07 ~ 4:14

OK's beginnings had become 17. _____ but it didn't really matter anymore the word was embedded in our language. Today, we use it as the ultimate "neutral 18. _____."

10 4:56 ~ 5:13

Which might be why OK was arguably the first word spoken when humans 19. _____ on the moon. Not bad for a 20. _____ joke from the 1830s.

Unit | 10

Discussion Question 1

Should we actively intervene to promote standard and correct language in order to unite our society for as long as possible, or should we minimize interference and let language evolve naturally as people use it comfortably? What is your opinion? Why do you think so?

Discussion Question 2

On January 2, 2024, at Haneda Airport in Japan, a fatal incident occurred in which a Coast Guard aircraft collided with a Japan Airlines aircraft. The air traffic controller said, "You're number one for takeoff," which means that the aircraft has the highest priority for takeoff among those waiting. While the Coast Guard aircraft pilot misunderstood "You are cleared for takeoff as number one" and entered the runway, he collided with the Japan Airlines passenger plane, which was landing, resulting in the deaths of five crew members.

Some argue that abbreviations used in specialized fields should be banned from everyday use. However, others argue that mandatory reviews should be conducted to avoid confusion with everyday language when creating abbreviations for specialized fields.

What are your thoughts on this? Why do you think so?

Unit | 10

Watch the part of the video and choose the correct answers.

01 How does "OK" become one of the most recognizable words?
- A its historical significance
- B its frequent use in technology
- C its global popularity

02 How many different misspelled abbreviations are mentioned in the video?
- A 2
- B 4
- C 6

03 How did the abbreviation "OK" gain popularity beyond Boston in the 1830s?
- A It was endorsed by influential intellectuals.
- B It was adopted by US newspapers.
- C It was popularized through telegraphic manuals

04 Why were "OK Clubs" formed during Van Buren's 1840 campaign?
- A to promote a new political ideology
- B to mock his opponents
- C to emphasize his hometown roots

05 What happened to other misspelled abbreviations from the 1830s?
- A They evolved into different words.
- B They fell out of fashion and were forgotten.
- C They were also standardized in telegraphic communication.

06 Why was "OK" particularly suitable for telegraphic communication?
- A It represented a standardized message format.
- B Its abbreviation was easy to transmit and understand.
- C It was universally recognized as a greeting.

07 What was the main objective of replacing hard Cs with Ks in advertising?
- A to create a visual appeal
- B to simplify spelling
- C to promote cultural unity

08 Why do some people believe that "OK" comes from the Choctaw word 'okeh'?
- A similar sound and meaning
- B popularized by Native American culture
- C adopted by early American settlers

09 According to the video, what is the ultimate function of "OK" in modern language?
- A to express detailed approval
- B to acknowledge information without evaluation
- C to replace other forms of greetings and farewells

10 What does the phrase "Not bad for a corny joke from the 1830s" mean in the video?
- A It criticizes the use of jokes in the 1830s.
- B It implies "OK" was always serious.
- C It highlights how "OK" became widely used despite its silly origins.

UNIT 11 — The History of Gun Control in Texas

Video title: Why can't prices just stay the same?
This unit is based on the YouTube content as stated above.

Heads-up

VOCABULARY

Match the vocabulary on the left with their definitions on the right.

01	mass shooting	**A**	the power of a president or governor to reject a proposed law
02	reform	**B**	a shooting incident in which multiple people are killed or injured
03	enact	**C**	relating to the principles or provisions of a constitution
04	governor	**D**	projectiles and their casings, used in firearms
05	ammunition	**E**	laws to regulate the manufacture, sale, possession, and use of firearms and ammunition
06	constitutional	**F**	passed or made into law
07	veto	**G**	laws that restrict local or state government cooperation with federal authorities
08	gun control	**H**	the elected head of a state government who can play a significant role in law-making
09	Second Amendment	**I**	the systematic process of making significant changes or improvements to laws or policies
10	sanctuary law	**J**	part of the US Constitution that protects the right of individuals to keep and bear arms

EXPRESSION

Unit | 11

Watch the video and fill in the blanks with correct expressions.

> **A** went nowhere **B** in the aftermath of **C** vocal about **D** opened fire **E** still in control
> **F** there's times **G** manage to **H** speaking out **I** set off **J** in response to

01 0:11 ~ 0:18

On May 18th, 2018, a gunman entered a high school in Santa Fe, Texas and _____.

02 0:35 ~ 0:40

And then finally, Scot _____ find me.

03 2:40 ~ 2:48

A state like Texas would go more towards pro-gun policies _____ a gun shooting.

04 3:39 ~ 3:50

In 1994, Texas elected a new governor: George W Bush who made it legal to carry a concealed gun his first year in office and _____ a trend in the state that's continued for decades.

05 4:38 ~ 4:49

Flo and Scot were also pushing for legislation _____ Santa Fe like laws that would hold parents accountable if their guns were used by their children to harm people.

06 5:39 ~ 5:45

But in the end, these proposals, along with Abbot's openness to red flag laws _____.

07 6:27 ~ 6:40

After elections were over, with Republicans _____ in 2021 Texas passed "constitutional carry": there would no longer be a requirement for Texans to have a license or receive any training to openly carry handguns.

08 6:57 ~ 7:10

But as the Republican Party has gone further and further to the right on issues you get a fringe of the party that is much more _____ all kinds of issues, including gun rights.

09 8:51 ~ 8:55

And so I feel like I have to keep _____. I have to do what I can.

10 8:56 ~ 8:59

_____ when I just think I'm going to stop.

FILL IN THE BLANK

Unit | 11

Watch the video and fill in the blanks with the correct words.

01 0:11 ~ 0:29
On May 18th, 2018, a 1. _____ entered a high school in Santa Fe, Texas and opened fire. I look down and I realize in my pants I had bloody holes in my pants and I realized I'm 2. _____ .

02 0:41 ~ 0:51
For four years, Flo and Scot have told their story over and over to push for new laws that could prevent 3. _____ . It's made them part of a 4. _____ conversation on guns in the US.

03 2:03 ~ 2:11
State 5. _____ controlled by Democrats were more likely to pass tighter gun laws. Republican-controlled states typically 6. _____ gun laws.

04 2:15 ~ 2:29
Mass shootings didn't have any 7. _____ significant effect on the number of laws passed by Democrats. While for Republican legislatures a mass shooting roughly doubles the number of laws 8. _____ that loosen gun restrictions in the next year.

05 2:40 ~ 2:49
A state like Texas would go more towards 9. _____ in the aftermath of a gun shooting. Texas has some of the loosest gun laws in the 10. _____ .

06 3:39 ~ 3:50
In 1994, Texas elected a new 11. _____ : George W Bush who made it legal to carry a 12. _____ gun his first year in office and set off a trend in the state that's continued for decades.

07 4:06 ~ 4:18
In 2017, a gunman killed 26 people at First Baptist Church in Sutherland Springs. Within two years, Texas made it 13. _____ to carry weapons in places of 14. _____ .

08 6:27 ~ 6:40
After elections were over, with Republicans still in control in 2021 Texas passed "15. _____ ":   there would no longer be a requirement for Texans to have a license or receive any training to 16. _____ carry handguns.

09 7:11 ~ 7:21
In recent years, a better organized 17. _____ movement has seen more success with tightening laws in some states. But the movement to expand gun 18. _____ isn't stopping.

10 8:26 ~ 8:47
In June 2022, in the aftermath of the Uvalde shooting in Texas President Biden signed the most significant federal 19. _____ in 30 years. One thing it does is incentivize states to pass red flag laws. But it can't make them do it. That power 20. _____ the states.

DISCUSSION

Read the following questions and share your answers in class.

Discussion Question 1

Many Americans own guns to protect themselves and their families from crime. Conversely, the United States leads the world in the number of gun-related incidents. What are your thoughts on gun ownership? Why do you think so?

Discussion Question 2

According to U.S. estimates, civilians own between 300 million and 400 million guns. On average, more than 45,000 people die from gun-related accidents each year. To reduce gun-related victims, Democrats insist that gun ownership be regulated by law. On the other hand, Republicans insist on easing restrictions on gun ownership and use. What do you think? Why do you think so?

Unit | 11

Watch the part of the video and choose the correct answers.

01 What legislative changes have Flo and Scot advocated for?
  A loosening gun laws B tightening gun control legislation
  C advocating for constitutional carry

02 Which political party tends to pass tighter gun laws in response to mass shootings?
  A Democrats B Republicans C both parties are equally likely

03 What change in Texas gun laws occurred under Governor George W. Bush in 1994?
  A Red flag laws were enacted. B Background checks were tightened.
  C Concealed carry became legal.

04 As discussed in the video, what does "constitutional carry" mean?
  A carrying firearms in public places without a license or training
  B Strict background checks C banning assault rifles nationwide

05 What did the 2002 statistic about state control indicate?
  A Divided control made passing new laws challenging.
  B Unified control made law passage easier.
  C beside two major parties, multiple parties controlled each state.

06 What federal gun law did President Biden enact in June 2022?
  A He signed a bill to tighten background checks nationwide.
  B He vetoed a state law on constitutional carry.
  C He encouraged states to adopt red flag laws through incentives.

07 What does the video suggest about the influence of state-level politics on gun laws?
  A States have no autonomy in gun legislation due to federal oversight.
  B States often replicate successful laws passed in other states.
  C Local municipalities, not state governments, solely determine gun laws.

08 Which constitutional right frequently comes up in discussions about gun control?
  A Right to privacy B Right to free speech C Right to bear arms

09 What role do "sanctuary laws" play in gun legislation?
  A facilitate federal enforcement B restrict local cooperation with federal gun laws
  C allow open carry in designated areas.

10 In the context of gun legislation, what is a veto primarily used for?
  A to bypass state legislatures B to prevent the passage of proposed gun laws
  C to encourage bipartisan compromise on gun issues

UNIT 12 — The Colonial Legacy in Jakarta

Video title: Why Jakarta is sinking
This unit is based on the YouTube content as stated above.

Heads-up

VOCABULARY

Unit | 12

Match the vocabulary on the left with their definitions on the right.

01 descended — **A** to release air or gas from something, causing it to shrink or collapse.

02 aquifer — **B** having small holes that allow liquids or gases to pass through

03 porous — **C** separated or set apart from others

04 deflates — **D** an underground layer of rock, sediment, or soil that yields water

05 colonial — **E** originating or occurring naturally in a particular place

06 outnumbered — **F** relating to or characteristic of a colony or colonies

07 deteriorate — **G** something, such as sewer that has not undergone necessary or expected processing

08 untreated — **H** having more people or things than another group

09 indigenous — **I** to become worse in quality or condition over time

10 segregated — **J** moved or fell downward from a higher to a lower level

Unit | 12

EXPRESSION

Watch the video and fill in the blanks with correct expressions.

> **A** at a fast pace **B** so far **C** at risk **D** left behind **E** sit on
> **F** rule over **G** no other choice but **H** up to **I** running out **J** prone to

01 1:24 ~ 1:35
Many residents here are fishermen, who need to live by the coast to make a living, but, further inland, Jakarta's more than 10 million residents are also _____.

02 1:42 ~ 1:45
Jakarta _____ a swampy plain, on low coastal land.

03 2:46 ~ 2:51
For decades, Jakarta has been developing _____, and is now covered in concrete.

04 3:01 ~ 3:11
It's gotten so bad that in coastal areas _____ flooding, like the fishing community Muara Baru, people have built makeshift bridges to move through their neighborhoods.

05 4:28 ~ 4:40
They began to _____ the Indonesian, Chinese, Indian, and Arab people who had lived there for centuries, and built their new city in the Dutch style, with narrow townhouses along a grid of canals.

06 7:55 ~ 8:04
The legacy they _____ was a sprawling city, built on marshland, and segregated by water access, that, now, Jakartans had to deal with.

07 8:31 ~ 8:37
Many of the people without access to piped water have _____ to keep pumping groundwater to survive.

08 9:10 ~ 9:14
But _____, only these 10 kilometers have been reinforced.

09 9:41 ~ 9:44
But this project could take _____ 30 years to complete.

10 10:28 ~ 10:30
But time is _____.

FILL IN THE BLANK

Unit | 12

Watch the video and fill in the blanks with the correct words.

01 0:39 ~ 0:49
Jakarta is sinking. And it's been sinking for 1. _____. These blue areas show just how much the city has sunk since the 2. _____.

02 0:56 ~ 1:13
Most of the sinking happens here, in the north coast, where Jakarta meets the 3. _____. Here, the land is sinking by about 25 cm a year, 4. _____ the area, damaging homes, and upending people's lives, over and over again.

03 3:12 ~ 3:25
Combined with 5. _____ rise, it's also made floods during 6. _____ and rainy seasons much more dangerous. Like in 2007, when Jakarta experienced one of the worst floods in its modern history.

04 4:14 ~ 4:27
In the 1600s, when European powers were 7. _____ the world, the 8. _____ took over what was then the port town of Jayakarta. They razed it to the ground, and in its place, built Batavia: a headquarters for their growing empire.

05 5:16 ~ 5:30
If you look closely, you'll notice that there aren't many 9. _____ between the two sides, or between the blocks. This was by design. The Dutch were 10. _____. So, in order to control the local population, they divided it.

06 5:47 ~ 5:59
Because the Dutch didn't properly maintain the canals, they began to 11. _____, and sediment from earthquakes blocked the flow of water. The water in the canals turned 12. _____, and soon, deadly.

07 6:21 ~ 6:29
But, despite the death and disease, the Dutch continued to leave the canals 13. _____. Instead, they began to use 14. _____.

08 8:05 ~ 8:21
Over the next decades, Jakarta's 15. _____ skyrocketed. More people required more housing, more stores, and more streets. And the city expanded fast. But its 16. _____ still doesn't serve the majority of the city.

09 10:03 ~ 10:13
Jakarta will continues to sink until 17. _____ stops being pumped. And groundwater will continue to be pumped until the government provides an 18. _____. This has been done before.

10 10:54 ~ 11:04
Jakarta is sinking into the sea. And, until its government 19. _____ how to provide clean, piped water for its citizens, that will continue to be its 20. _____.

DISCUSSION

Unit | 12

Read the following questions and share your answers in class.

Discussion Question 1

Urbanization brings numerous benefits, such as economic growth, improved safety, and enhanced access to infrastructure. However, rapid and unplanned urbanization has detrimental effects, leading to sinking cities such as Jakarta and the proliferation of slum areas in cities like Mumbai and Manila.

Should countries or central governments prioritize urban development to mitigate infrastructure deficiencies and achieve economic growth, or should they focus on sustainable urbanization to balance development and conservation? What do you think? Why do you think so?

Discussion Question 2

Some argue for restricting resource development to combat global warming and climate change. This means reducing fossil fuel use and transitioning to renewable energy to cut carbon emissions. They warn that unchecked development will worsen climate change, causing severe natural disasters and ecosystem damage and threatening human survival. Others advocate increasing resource development for human survival. Energy and resources are crucial for modern society, supporting population growth and economic development. They argue that limiting development could hinder economic progress, leading to poverty and energy shortages. Thus, there's a call for sustainable resource strategies.

What is your stance on the debate surrounding resource development, climate change, and human survival? What do you think? Why do you think so?

QUIZ

Unit | 12

Watch the part of the video and choose the correct answers.

01 What factors contribute to Jakarta's sinking issue?
- **A** industrial pollution
- **B** frequent earthquakes
- **C** rapid urbanization and groundwater pumping

02 Why is groundwater pumping a critical issue in Jakarta?
- **A** because it accelerates urbanization processes
- **B** because it raises sea levels.
- **C** because it causes land subsidence and sinking.

03 How does the video explain the success of the government's seawall project?
- **A** successful completion of 120 km of seawalls
- **B** immediate halt of Jakarta's sinking process.
- **C** partial completion and ongoing challenges

04 How did Dutch colonial rule affect Jakarta's water management?
- **A** introduction of advanced irrigation techniques
- **B** segregation of water access based on socio-economic status
- **C** implementation of sustainable water policies

05 What lesson should Jakarta learn from other cities like Tokyo, Taipei, and Shanghai?
- **A** strict water rationing policies
- **B** sustainable urban development practices
- **C** relocating urban populations to rural areas

06 How might moving the capital to Borneo affect Jakarta's sinking?
- **A** accelerating coastal erosion
- **B** relieving population pressure and reducing sinking
- **C** intensifying infrastructure development in Jakarta

07 How does urbanization worsen Jakarta's sinking?
- **A** by reducing groundwater pumping rates
- **B** by increasing green spaces
- **C** by adding weight and stress to the soil

08 What are some socio-economic impacts of Jakarta's sinking on its residents?
- **A** improved living conditions in coastal areas
- **B** displacement of vulnerable communities
- **C** enhanced access to recreational facilities

09 During colonial rule, why did the Dutch implement segregated quarters in Jakarta?
- **A** to maintain cultural diversity
- **B** to control and manage local populations
- **C** to facilitate economic trade and commerce

10 How long did the Dutch rule Indonesia before its independence was recognized?
- **A** less than 100 years
- **B** approximately 200 years
- **C** more than 300 years

UNIT 13 The New Microchip Cold War

Video title: Why China is losing the microchip war
This unit is based on the YouTube content as stated above.

Heads-up

VOCABULARY

Unit | 13

Match the vocabulary on the left with their definitions on the right.

01 semiconductor

A most advanced and innovative stage of development in a particular field

02 exponential rate

B a material that has electrical conductivity between that of a conductor and an insulator

03 supply chain

C critical points that the flow can be restricted or halted, causing delays and inefficiencies

04 Moore's Law

D the illegal appropriation of intellectual property

05 geopolitical

E a rate of growth that increases rapidly in proportion to the growing total number or size

06 cutting edge

F financial assistance provided by the government to support or promote economic sectors

07 chokepoints

G the network involved in delivering a product or service from suppliers to customers

08 IP theft

H when an action has the opposite effect of what was intended

09 backfire

I a law that the number of microchip transistors doubles about every two years

10 subsidies

J relating to politics, especially international relations, as influenced by geographical factors

Unit | 13

EXPRESSION

Watch the video and fill in the blanks with correct expressions.

> **A** lagging behind **B** zero sum **C** dealt a significant blow **D** cut off **E** allege
> **F** keep racing ahead **G** pick sides **H** at a cost **I** back in time **J** their choice

01 0:18 ~ 0:26
US and ASML lawyers would later _____ that Yu recruited other ASML engineers to his US company that they brought with them stolen information about AMSL's machine.

02 0:27 ~ 0:29
and that it was all _____ the Chinese government.

03 3:57 ~ 4:02
But while the US and its allies were pushing the limits of chip technology China was _____.

04 4:03 ~ 4:12
In addition to the US blocking it from accessing chips during the Cold War many of China's brightest scientists and engineers had been _____ by the dictator Mao Zedong during the 60s and 70s.

05 4:49 ~ 4:53
And China's leaders concluded quite understandably, that this was a risk they were _____ continue to take.

06 7:36 ~ 7:39
These bans nearly bankrupted ZTE and _____ to Huawei.

07 8:07 ~ 8:21
These export controls represented a really clear shift away from the view that ultimately trade and tax exchanges with China were fundamentally positive sum to a much more _____ view of the technological competition.

08 8:33 ~ 8:35
All to enable the U.S. to keep _____.

09 9:29 ~ 9:31
So far, they've signaled they'll _____ China.

10 9:38 ~ 9:43
Asking them to _____ in what looks a lot like a new Cold War.

FILL IN THE BLANK

Unit | 13

Watch the video and fill in the blanks with the correct words.

01 0:39 ~ 0:46
But China's effort has increasingly locked it in a 1. _____ with the United States. This isn't about market share. This isn't about tariffs. This is about 2. _____.

02 1:20 ~ 1:40
So since the early 1960s, semiconductors have 3. _____ at an exponential rate. This is Chris Miller, author of Chip War. The founder of Intel, Gordon Moore predicted in 1965 that the computing power produced by a single chip would 4. _____ every year or so and that rate has held true roughly up to the present.

03 1:41 ~ 1:48
The first companies 5. _____ making chips were in the US where they really just had one main customer: 6. _____.

04 2:36 ~ 2:55
But by the late 1960s, they realized they could make a lot more money designing chips for civilian products like 7. _____. They just had to make a lot more of them and a lot less expensively. So many chip companies moved their manufacturing and assembly to factories in Japan, Taiwan, South Korea and Hong Kong where 8. _____ was cheaper.

05 3:28 ~ 3:47
In the 1970s and 80s Toshiba in Japan and Samsung in South Korea began designing and manufacturing chips that 9. _____ the Americans'. In the 1990s, a Taiwanese company, TSMC got so good at manufacturing chips that many companies in the US stopped doing it. It meant that U.S. companies were not the only ones who could make the most 10. _____ chips anymore.

06 4:16 ~ 4:27
By the 1990s, 11. _____ was over. The US had become friendlier with China and it had lifted most of its export controls. And so China 12. _____ many chip companies to move their assembly operations to China.

07 4:28 ~ 4:36
And by the 2000s, China 13. _____ this end of the supply chain. But China was importing more and more chips to feed its assembly industry and it put them in a 14. _____ position.

08 5:33 ~ 5:42
The problem is, only a few companies in the world are involved in making them and 15. _____ are in China. To start, only 3 American companies make the 16. _____ to design advanced chips.

09 6:39 ~ 6:58
In order to eventually decrease its reliance on this foreign supply chain China was identifying 17. _____ like ASML and copying them. But the plan backfired. And this has really 18. _____ the US government, other governments, and caused them to take China's subsidies as a more security focused issue rather than just an economic issue.

10 8:49 ~ 9:02
But this has also put extraordinary 19. _____ on another conflict between the two countries. Since 1949, China has viewed Taiwan as a breakaway province and has vowed to reunite with it, even threatening invasion. The US has 20. _____ to protect Taiwan.

76 | HiEnglish

DISCUSSION

Unit | 13

Read the following questions and share your answers in class.

Discussion Question 1

In today's world, possessing technology can be a significant asset, but transferring it to rival entities or other countries can lead to substantial financial and legal penalties. Despite this, incidents of industrial technology theft are increasing, as seen in South Korea, where cases rose from 14 in 2019 to 23 in 2023 amidst the US-China technology rivalry.

Why do you think attempts to steal industrial technology are increasing? Is it because current penalties are not strong enough, or are potential rewards after theft perceived as much greater? If so, what would the appropriate punishments be for IP theft? What do you think? Why do you think so?

Discussion Question 2

China has long been producing semiconductors via imports at the end of the supply chain. The United States controls the supply chain through ties with allied countries and companies. Still, China aims for semiconductor self-sufficiency with Communist Party support and intends to acquire TSMC through military action. In the dispute between China's ambitious semiconductor production plans and the U.S.'s establishment of global order in the semiconductor supply chain, Samsung and ASML might have to choose between pursuing financial opportunities through China or strengthening their alliance with the United States.

Do you think China's semiconductor investment will succeed? Or do you anticipate that U.S. supply chain control plans will be maintained? What do you think? Why do you think so?

Unit | 13

Watch the part of the video and choose the correct answers.

01 How have semiconductors evolved since the early 1960s, according to the video?
- **A** They have improved at an exponential rate
- **B** They have decreased complexity.
- **C** They have remained stagnant in performance

02 What does Moore's Law predict about the computing power of chips?
- **A** The size of chips will double every year.
- **B** The cost of manufacturing chips will decrease every two years.
- **C** The computing power produced by a single chip will double approximately every year.

03 Why did Toshiba and Samsung become key players in the 70s and 80s?
- **A** Software advancements
- **B** result from long investments in mechanical engineering
- **C** Competitive chip design and manufacturing

04 What challenges did China face in semiconductor self-sufficiency?
- **A** difficulty in attracting skilled engineers
- **B** dependence on US export controls
- **C** lack of government support for the semiconductor industry

05 How did the US government's actions impact Chinese tech companies?
- **A** enhanced their global market share
- **B** created opportunities for collaboration
- **C** led to financial hardships and operational challenges

06 Why are ASML and TSMC considered critical choke points?
- **A** control global distribution
- **B** produce essential manufacturing equipment
- **C** Only chip manufacturers

07 How has China viewed Taiwan since 1949?
- **A** independent sovereign state
- **B** a part of its territory
- **C** no interest at all

08 How does semiconductor technology relate to national security?
- **A** promotes global trade
- **B** potential vulnerabilities
- **C** environmental concerns

09 What resulted from China's reduced reliance on foreign semiconductors?
- **A** reliance on imported semiconductor materials
- **B** decreased investment in domestic semiconductor companies
- **C** development of advanced semiconductor manufacturing capabilities

10 What is Taiwan's role in the semiconductor industry?
- **A** Taiwanese companies manufacture a large portion of the world's semiconductors.
- **B** Taiwan owns the majority of semiconductor patents globally.
- **C** Taiwan has imposed strict export controls on semiconductor technology.

UNIT 14 — Unveiling Media Deception

Video title: Why cheating is allowed on game shows
This unit is based on the YouTube content as stated above.

Heads-up

VOCABULARY

Unit | 14

Match the vocabulary on the left with their definitions on the right.

01 scandal
02 debut
03 rigged
04 contestants
05 deceitfully
06 testimony
07 Communications Act
08 controversy
09 statute
10 enforcement

A. a law enacted to regulate interstate and foreign communication by wire and radio

B. the first public appearance or performance of something or someone

C. a publicized incident that causes public outrage or censure

D. a formal written or spoken statement given in a court of law or before an official body

E. in a way that involves deceiving or misleading others

F. individuals who participate in a competition or contest

G. a prolonged public dispute, debate, or argument concerning a matter of opinion

H. a formal written law enacted by a legislative body

I. manipulated or controlled dishonestly or unfairly to produce a desired outcome

J. the act of compelling observance of or compliance with a law, rule, or obligation

EXPRESSION

Unit | 14

Watch the video and fill in the blanks with correct expressions.

> A topping ratings B in charge C a bitterly high price D in violation E family friendly celebrity
> F pure fiction G respond to H pled guilty I the less said the better J on the cover

01 1:44 ~ 1:50

It was sponsored by Revlon and was a fabulously successful TV show _____ with 16 million viewers.

02 1:59 ~ 2:09

These shows included Dotto a game where contestants answered trivia questions to unlock a connect-the-dots puzzle. _____. And Twenty One.

03 2:25 ~ 2:34

The show and trend peaked in 1957 when Time magazine put long-running quiz champ Charles Van Doren _____.

04 2:45 ~ 2:54

Van Doren became a _____. TV's own health restoring antidote to Elvis Presley as part of the literary Van Doren clan.

05 4:15 ~ 4:24

It is one thing to arouse and hold the attention of the viewing public by programs which are openly and avowedly _____.

06 5:23 ~ 5:29

But his statement is a rueful and moving realization that for his wealth and fame he paid _____.

07 5:39 ~ 5:44

Though he and others _____ of perjury in earlier testimony he was freed.

08 6:04 ~ 6:08

The FCC was _____ and rigging the game show was a federal crime.

09 8:30 ~ 8:37

You can shoot something for broadcast but as long as it doesn't actually air, you're not _____.

10 9:30 ~ 9:34

The Mr. Beast team did not _____ our multiple requests for comment.

FILL IN THE BLANK

Unit | 14

Watch the video and fill in the blanks with the correct words.

01 0:48 ~ 1:00
Around half of Mr. Beast's videos are now 1. _____. Their questionable reality is part of a history that goes back to a 2. _____ in the 1950s.

02 1:17 ~ 1:28
In the 1940s, television had begun 3. _____ across the nation. And by 1955, a game show called "The $64,000 Question" 4. _____ on CBS.

03 1:51 ~ 2:05
Almost half of all houses that owned TVs were watching it. It started a quiz show 5. _____. These shows included Dotto a game where 6. _____ answered trivia questions to unlock a connect-the-dots puzzle.

04 3:26 ~ 3:39
In summer of '58, Dotto went blotto. The show was canceled after a contestant found an answer filled notebook 7. _____. A slew of shows were implicated in "8. _____" over the next few years, including Twenty One.

05 4:04 ~ 4:13
The producers claimed Stempel was 9. _____ them. The 10. _____ Subcommittee on Legislative Oversight began hearings on the quiz shows.

06 5:30 ~ 5:38
The investigations resulted in Van Doren 11. _____ his job as a Today Show correspondent and in the 12. _____ of other quiz shows.

07 5:44 ~ 6:03
But more importantly, the Communications Act of 1934 was 13. _____ to include prohibited practices in case of contests of intellectual knowledge or chance making it unlawful with intent to 14. _____ the listening or viewing public with up to a year of imprisonment.

08 6:32 ~ 6:46
The long running show Survivor made its debut in 2000. Contestants competed in challenges, but crucially elimination occurred via 15. _____ at Tribal Council. In 2001, an original Survivor cast member claimed the show was 16. _____.

09 7:45 ~ 7:57
The planned 2009 show cast kids as quiz competitors to adults. One 17. _____ to the FCC said their child had been registered as a calculus expert but was suddenly 18. _____ to music theory.

10 8:30 ~ 8:48
You can shoot something for broadcast but as long as it doesn't actually 19. _____, you're not in violation. And the time line of game show investigations 20. _____ with a change in consumption options. Game shows being real was possibly just a window in time.

DISCUSSION

Read the following questions and share your answers in class.

Discussion Question 1

Recently, producers of a domestic idol audition program manipulated rankings. Also, broadcasters expose their company's advertisements as if they are not advertisements.

Should producers have the right to deceive viewers purposefully? What do you think? Why do you think so?

Discussion Question 2

Some argue that fabricated reality content loses credibility with viewers, leading to decreased viewership. Therefore, it's critical to monitor the authenticity of media content constantly. Conversely, some argue that producing media content that viewers do not watch is no longer possible.

Therefore, we should allow a certain degree of fiction to produce reality content. What is your opinion? Why do you think so?

Unit | 14

Watch the part of the video and choose the correct answers.

01 What historical event does the video compare to Mr. Beast's clip?
  A MTV's launch **B** Survivor's controversy **C** the 1950s' quiz shows scandals

02 Why was Elvis Presley mentioned in the video?
  A to compare his popularity with that of Charles Van Doren
  B to highlight his influence on quiz show production
  C to discuss his involvement in quiz show scandals

03 How did the Survivor controversy connect to quiz show laws from the 1950s?
  A A contestant cheated by looking up answers, like cheating on a quiz show.
  B Producers were accused of manipulating votes and raising questions about old quiz show.
  C Contestants were bribed to lose, similar to early quiz show practices.

04 What was the relationship between Charles Van Doren and Herbert Stempel?
  A fair competition **B** Van Doren replaced Stempel
  C exposed producer manipulation

05 What is the changes in audience perceptions of game shows and online content?
  A more gullible now than in the 1950s **B** less interested in game shows
  C more skeptical and aware that much of what they see may be fake

06 What do 1950s quiz show scandals and modern reality TV controversies share?
  A Both involve producer deception. **B** The scandals focused on financial fraud.
  C Both include manipulated outcomes, often avoiding regulation due to media changes.

07 Why did the FCC investigate the planned Fox game show 'Our Little Genius?'
  A The show was canceled for being too controversial.
  B Producers provided answers, but the show never aired.
  C The show aired without issue after the investigation.

08 How did Twenty One's producers manipulate outcomes?
  A They provided answers. **B** They used actors.
  C They edited footage to change outcomes.

09 Why was the term "hemidemisemiquaver" mentioned in the script?
  A It refers to a popular dance move used in game shows of the 1950s.
  B It describes a quiz question format used in early reality TV programs.
  C It is a musical term referenced in a game show controversy.

10 What does "Game shows being real was possibly just a window in time" imply?
  A always authentic **B** brief period of belief in authenticity **C** consistent authenticity

UNIT 15 — From Orchards to Tech Powerhouse

Video title: Why Silicon Valley is here
This unit is based on the YouTube content as stated above.

Heads-up

VOCABULARY

Match the vocabulary on the left with their definitions on the right.

01 public welfare — **A** a person or entity that rents or leases a property from a landlord

02 proximity — **B** to officially register or sign up for something, such as a course, program, or membership

03 tenant — **C** the well-being of the general public in terms of health, safety, and prosperity

04 corporate — **D** a reference to something indirectly or metaphorically

05 enroll — **E** the state of being near or close in distance

06 solicitation — **F** funding provided to startups or small businesses with perceived long-term growth potential

07 venture capital — **G** relating to a corporation or large company

08 allusion — **H** required or necessary for a particular purpose or achievement

09 dotcom — **I** the act of seeking or asking for something

10 requisite — **J** relating to companies operating primarily on the internet

EXPRESSION

Unit | 15

Watch the video and fill in the blanks with correct expressions.

> Ⓐ the Bay Area Ⓑ a short drive away Ⓒ land rich Ⓓ split off Ⓔ eggheads
> Ⓕ iconic name Ⓖ powered forward Ⓗ credited with Ⓘ peon group Ⓙ bearby

01 1:28 ~ 1:31

Built from the land grant of Leland Stanford the university was _____.

02 1:48 ~ 1:54

Frederick Terman was a professor of electrical engineering at Stanford as well as an _____ in radio science.

03 3:40 ~ 3:44

He proudly clipped this article about faculty _____ becoming millionaires.

04 4:38 ~ 4:42

Terman explicitly said this cycle would not only affect _____ but the national labor market.

05 4:59 ~ 5:04

Terman said if the Midwest continues to plod along in electronics it is destined to become the _____.

06 5:33 ~ 5:39

And later, _____ in Stanford Industrial Park where HP secured a 40-acre site.

07 5:45 ~ 5:51

William Shockley's Shockley Semiconductor Laboratory is widely _____ starting the Silicon semiconductor boom.

08 6:10 ~ 6:22

Employees split off Shockley to form Fairchild Semiconductors in Mountain View and then those employees _____ to form Intel locally and so on and so on.

09 6:42 ~ 6:49

As venture capital grew in the 1960s _____ Sandhill Road was an obvious location due to its proximity to the Stanford epicenter.

10 7:21 ~ 7:24

And from Netscape on _____ in the first dotcom boom.

FILL IN THE BLANK

Unit | 15

Watch the video and fill in the blanks with the correct words.

01 0:28 ~ 0:44
During World War II, American engineer Vannevar Bush basically led wartime 1. _____.
And in 1945 he published an essay called "Science: The Endless Frontier". Bush reported to President Roosevelt that the 2. _____ is still vigorous within this nation.

02 1:19 ~ 1:31
That was paired with proximity to Stanford University the college that had 3. _____ land resources than cash. Built from the land 4. _____ of Leland Stanford the university was land rich.

03 2:23 ~ 2:30
Stanford developed the Stanford Shopping Mall to help 5. _____ their lack of cash. It's still 6. _____ by the university today.

04 2:59 ~ 3:08
But it was more than just a 7. _____ on the university's land. From the beginning, Terman imagined 8. _____. Stanford to companies to Stanford to companies.

05 3:28 ~ 3:39
He 9. _____ this in many ways including allowing professors to spend time in corporate roles and get corporate 10. _____ and helping companies enroll employees as Stanford students.

06 4:38 ~ 4:42
Terman 11. _____ said this cycle would not only affect the Bay Area but the 12. _____ labor market.

07 4:59 ~ 5:07
Terman said if 13. _____ continues to plod along in electronics, it is destined to become the peon group in the nation's 14. _____ industry.

08 5:40 ~ 5:56
Stanford Industrial Park became a 15. _____ for any successful industry that might emerge. William Shockley's Shockley Semiconductor Laboratory is widely credited with starting the Silicon 16. _____ boom and Fred Terman solicited Shockley to start his business in the Valley.

09 6:42 ~ 6:58
As venture capital grew in the 1960s bearby Sandhill Road was an obvious location due to its proximity to the Stanford 17. _____. By 1971, journalist Don Hoefler former publicist for Fairchild Semiconductor labeled the region 18. _____ for a series of articles.

10 7:47 ~ 7:56
And today's Silicon Valley has fewer 19. _____ but it remains in all its 20. _____ ways a Valley of Heart's Delight.

88| HiEnglish

DISCUSSION

Read the following questions and share your answers in class.

Discussion Question 1

Many universities have established industry-university cooperation centers and implemented initiatives such as capstone courses and employment-linked programs. However, many business leaders and university presidents in Korea believe that industry-academia collaboration requires improvement and lags behind leading nations in technology and innovation.

Which aspect, industry or academia, requires more effort to improve this situation? What do you think? Why do you think so?

Discussion Question 2

Some argue that developing industrial parks and companies through voluntary investment and collaboration with academic institutions like Stanford University boosts local economies and technological innovation.
Others believe that taxing research activities and strategically relocating promising companies is more beneficial for local economic growth and technological advancement.

What do you think? Why do you think so?

QUIZ

Unit | 15

Watch the part of the video and choose the correct answers.

01 What was the Santa Clara Valley once known as?
 A Valley of Innovation   B Valley of Riches   C Valley of Heart's Delight

02 What role did Vannevar Bush play during World War II?
 A an engineer led wartime R&D   B a farmer led agricultural innovations
 C a politician led government reforms

03 How did Stanford University's land resources compare to its cash resources?
 A more cash than land   B equal amounts of cash and land
 C greater land resources than cash

04 What was the primary purpose of developing the Stanford Industrial Park?
 A to create a residential area for faculty
 B to attract businesses and generate revenue for the university
 C to build a large commercial shopping center

05 What was the key concept behind Terman's envisioned cycle?
 A continuous flow of financial investments between Stanford and the tech industry
 B cyclical employment and educational exchanges between Stanford and local companies
 C permanent migration of Stanford graduates to other states

06 How did Terman integrate academic knowledge with industry practices?
 A by establishing a purely academic curriculum   B by restricting faculty engagement
 C by allowing professors to work in corporate roles

07 What would determine the future success of growth industries in the United States?
 A government regulations and policies
 B access to highly trained manpower from major universities
 C proximity to large markets

08 In the 1960s, how did the Bay Area compare to the Midwest in terms of electronics?
 A The Midwest was advancing faster in electronics than the Bay Area.
 B The Bay Area was predicted to be the leader, while the Midwest would fall behind.
 C Both regions were progressing at the same rate in electronics.

09 What was Shockley's role in Silicon Valley?
 A invented the first computer   B established the first software company in the Valley
 C founded Shockley Semiconductor Laboratory

10 When did Stanford Research Park expand to 700 acres?
 A by 1960   B by 1980   C by 2000

VOX ENGLISH

Answer Key

ANSWER

Unit 1 - The Secrets of Airplane Legroom

- **Vocabulary**
  1. D 2. A 3. C 4. B 5. E 6. I 7. G 8. F 9. J 10. H
- **Expression**
  1. B 2. D 3. E 4. A 5. C 6. F 7. J 8. G 9. I 10. H
- **Fill in the blank**
  1. seat pitch 2. measurements 3. room 4. spacious 5. luxurious
  6. exit row 7. goes down 8. amenities 9. bundled together 10. carry-on
  11. padding 12. space saving 13. coach 14. segmentation 15. self-select
  16. cramped 17. thrilled 18. in an emergency 19. at a cost 20. on a regular basis
- **Quiz**
  1. B 2. A 3. B 4. C 5. A 6. A 7. B 8. A 9. C 10. B

Unit 2 - Ukraine under Siege

- **Vocabulary**
  1. B 2. D 3. F 4. A 5. G 6. J 7. H 8. C 9. E 10. I
- **Expression**
  1. I 2. A 3. D 4. C 5. G 6. B 7. F 8. H 9. E 10. J
- **Fill in the blank**
  1. sovereign 2. identity 3. communist 4. democracies 5. declaring independence
  6. independent 7. wanted to join 8. becoming a member 9. Crimean Peninsula 10. captured
  11. conducting 12. became real 13. Ukrainian border 14. state of emergency 15. invasion
  16. spoken out 17. protests 18. opened their borders 19. economic sanctions 20. military aid
- **Quiz**
  1. B 2. B 3. A 4. A 5. B 6. B 7. B 8. B 9. A and C 10. B

Unit 3 - Navigating the Trade Highway

- **Vocabulary**
  1. B 2. D 3. F 4. I 5. H 6. J 7. E 8. A 9. C 10. G
- **Expression**
  1. G 2. A 3. F 4. D 5. I 6. E 7. C 8. B 9. J 10. H
- **Fill in the blank**
  1. risen 2. other goods 3. eliminate 4. illegal immigration 5. tariff-free
  6. overseas 7. three-quarters 8. before NAFTA 9. less to do with 10. more to do with
  11. layoffs 12. at NAFTA 13. American sourced parts 14. $16 an hour 15. on paper
  16. out of hand 17. leave 18. global market 19. cheap 20. pay the price
- **Quiz**
  1. A 2. B 3. C 4. A 5. A 6. B 7. B 8. B 9. B 10. B

ANSWER

Unit 4 - Breaking Phone Addiction

- **Vocabulary**
  1. B 2. J 3. C 4. F 5. G 6. I 7. A 8. D 9. H 10. E
- **Expression**
  1. C 2. A 3. F 4. I 5. G 6. B 7. E 8. H 9. J 10. D
- **Fill in the blank**
  1. engaged 2. tricks 3. social interaction 4. platform 5. replicate
  6. a conscious 7. bundling 8. stress 9. grayscale 10. sensitive
  11. redesigned 12. bubbles 13. distracting 14. tricked 15. home screens
  16. built-in 17. infinite 18. load 19. philosophical 20. genuinely worth
- **Quiz**
  1. B 2. C 3. A 4. C 5. A 6. B 7. B 8. B 9. A 10. A

Unit 5 - The Hidden Dangers of Sliding Sports

- **Vocabulary**
  1. B 2. A 3. D 4. F 5. E 6. H 7. C 8. J 9. I 10. G
- **Expression**
  1. J 2. A 3. C 4. D 5. F 6. G 7. E 8. H 9. I 10. B
- **Fill in the blank**
  1. the sliding sports 2. inevitability 3. retired 4. troubling symptoms 5. main driver
  6. sled head 7. little things 8. make up 9. look smooth 10. brain rattling
  11. average concussion 12. at its highest 13. vibrations 14. encounter 15. over-activation
  16. trauma 17. look after 18. per person 19. bodies 20. legislative
- **Quiz**
  1. B 2. C 3. A 4. C 5. A 6. A 7. A 8. C 9. B 10. C

Unit 6 - Inequality and Climate Change

- **Vocabulary**
  1. E 2. D 3. C 4. A 5. I 6. H 7. B 8. J 9. G 10. F
- **Expression**
  1. J 2. A 3. I 4. E 5. D 6. F 7. G 8. B 9. H 10. C
- **Fill in the blank**
  1. correlation 2. separate 3. Climate change 4. Urban development 5. hottest
  6. coolest 7. of course 8. designed to 9. surface temperature 10. coating
  11. cooling effect 12. trees 13. planting 14. canopy cover 15. urban forest
  16. private 17. maintaining 18. very low income 19. heaviest burdens, 20. withstand
- **Quiz**
  1. A 2. C 3. C 4. B 5. B 6. C 7. C 8. A 9. A 10. C

ANSWER

Unit 7 - Artificial Intelligence in Warfare

- **Vocabulary**
  1. G 2. B 3. J 4. E 5. F 6. D 7. C 8. I 9. H 10. A
- **Expression**
  1. H 2. C 3. E 4. F 5. I 6. A 7. G 8. J 9. B 10. D
- **Fill in the blank**
  1. destroyed 2. directed by 3. precision strikes 4. something different 5. AI systems
  6. bombing targets 7. produces 8. conjunction 9. civil pressure 10. power targets
  11. generate 12. often wrong 13. civilians 14. as high as 15. facts
  16. prediction 17. last step 18. Human approval 19. unwilling test 20. future
- **Quiz**
  1. B 2. A 3. B 4. C 5. C 6. B 7. C 8. B 9. B 10. C

Unit 8 - Impacts of Light on Sleep Cycles

- **Vocabulary**
  1. B 2. E 3. G 4. A 5. I 6. H 7. F 8. D 9. C 10. J
- **Expression**
  1. J 2. H 3. I 4. B 5. D 6. F 7. C 8. G 9. A 10. E
- **Fill in the blank**
  1. not supposed to 2. ignored 3. melatonin 4. timekeeper 5. bright light
  6. awake and alert 7. shift 8. sleepy 9. blue light 10. disrupting
  11. manipulate 12. spectrum 13. complicated 14. aspect 15. duration
  16. brightness 17. circadian 18. offset 19. hacks 20. factors
- **Quiz**
  1. B 2. B 3. C 4. A 5. B 6. C 7. B 8. A 9. C 10. B

Unit 9 - The Secret Behind the Shaky Inflation Rate

- **Vocabulary**
  1. C 2. E 3. B 4. I 5. I 6. A 7. D 8. F 9. H 10. J
- **Expression**
  1. I 2. G 3. H 4. D 5. B 6. A 7. J 8. E 9. F 10. C
- **Fill in the blank**
  1. high inflation 2. peaking at 3. stay at zero 4. central banks 5. arbitrary number
  6. economists 7. wage growth 8. reversed 9. supply chain 10. drove up
  11. demand 12. price growth 13. instead of 14. pretty good 15. pretty rare
  16. The Great Depression 17. avoid 18. inflation targets 19. at risk 20. higher
- **Quiz**
  1. A 2. C 3. B 4. B 5. C 6. B 7. C 8. B 9. B 10. C

ANSWER

Unit 10 - The Origin of the Word 'OK'

- **Vocabulary**
  1. H 2. C 3. E 4. A 5. J 6. B 7. G 8. F 9. D 10. I
- **Expression**
  1. I 2. E 3. F 4. J 5. D 6. A 7. C 8. G 9. H 10. B
- **Fill in the blank**
  1. two-letter 2. recognizable 3. misspelling 4. butchered 5. published
  6. insiders 7. supporters 8. press 9. vernacular 10. telegraph
  11. tap out 12. confused 13. communicate 14. letter K 15. rarity
  16. attention 17. obscure 18. affirmative 19. landed 20. corny
- **Quiz**
  1. C 2. B 3. B 4. C 5. B 6. B 7. A 8. A 9. B 10. B

Unit 11 - The History of Gun Control in Texas

- **Vocabulary**
  1. B 2. I 3. F 4. H 5. D 6. C 7. A 8. E 9. J 10. G
- **Expression**
  1. D 2. G 3. B 4. I 5. J 6. A 7. E 8. C 9. H 10. F
- **Fill in the blank**
  1. gunman 2. shot 3. mass shootings 4. recurring 5. legislatures
  6. loosened 7. statistically 8. enacted 9. pro-gun policies 10. Nation
  11. governor 12. concealed 13. legal 14. worship 15. constitutional
  16. openly 17. gun control 18. access 19. gun bill 20. still belongs to
- **Quiz**
  1. B 2. A 3. C 4. A 5. A 6. A 7. B 8. C 9. B 10. B

Unit 12 - The Colonial Legacy in Jakarta

- **Vocabulary**
  1. J 2. D 3. B 4. A 5. F 6. H 7. I 8. G 9. E 10. C
- **Expression**
  1. C 2. E 3. A 4. J 5. F 6. D 7. B 8. G 9. H 10. I
- **Fill in the blank**
  1. decades 2. 1970s 3. Java Sea 4. destabilizing 5. sea level
  6. high tide 7. colonizing 8. Dutch 9. bridges 10. Outnumbered
  11. deteriorate 12. stagnant 13. untreated 14. piped water 15. population
  16. water infrastructure 17. groundwater 18. alternative 19. figures out 20. reality
- **Quiz**
  1. C 2. C 3. C 4. B 5. B 6. A 7. C 8. B 9. B 10. C

ANSWER

Unit 13 - The New Microchip Cold War
- **Vocabulary**
  1. B 2. E 3. G 4. I 5. J 6. A 7. C 8. D 9. H 10. F
- **Expression**
  1. E 2. H 3. A 4. I 5. J 6. C 7. B 8. F 9. D 10. G
- **Fill in the blank**
  1. struggle 2. security 3. improved 4. double 5. dedicated to
  6. the US government 7. corporate 8. labor 9. rivaled, 10. advanced
  11. the Cold War 12. enticed 13. dominated 14. tricky 15. none
  16. software needed 17. chokepoints 18. angered 19. pressure 20. vowed
- **Quiz**
  1. A 2. C 3. C 4. B 5. C 6. B 7. B 8. B 9. C 10. A

Unit 14 - Unveiling Media Deception
- **Vocabulary**
  1. C 2. B 3. I 4. F 5. E 6. D 7. A 8. G 9. H 10. J
- **Expression**
  1. A 2. I 3. J 4. E 5. F 6. C 7. H 8. B 9. D 10. G
- **Fill in the blank**
  1. game shows 2. national scandal 3. advances 4. debuted 5. boom to
  6. contestants 7. backstage 8. quiz guilt 9. blackmailing 10. US House
  11. losing 12. cancellation 13. amended 14. deceive 15. vote
  16. rigged 17. complainant 18. switched 19. air 20. overlaps
- **Quiz**
  1. C 2. A 3. B 4. C 5. C 6. C 7. B 8. A 9. C 10. B

Unit 15 - From Orchards to Tech Powerhouse
- **Vocabulary**
  1. C 2. E 3. A 4. G 5. B 6. I 7. F 8. D 9. J 10. H
- **Expression**
  1. C 2. F 3. E 4. A 5. I 6. B 7. H 8. D 9. J 10. G
- **Fill in the blank**
  1. R&D 2. pioneer spirit 3. greater 4. grant 5. remedy
  6. leased 7. development 8. a new cycle 9. encouraged 10. paydays
  11. explicitly 12. national 13. the Midwest 14. electronics 15. platform
  16. semiconductor 17. epicenter 18. Silicon Valley 19. prunes 20. complicated
- **Quiz**
  1. C 2. A 3. C 4. B 5. B 6. C 7. B 8. B 9. C 10. C

High Five 1, 2

MP3 무료 다운로드
무료 동영상 강의
[포켓캠퍼스 무료 동영상 강의 & 무료 팟캐스트]

주요포인트

학습대상	기초부터 차근차근 영어회화를 배우려는 임직원
기대효과	영어 어순의 원리를 배움으로서 구조 있는 영어 문장 말하기
교재의 차별화	배운 표현들의 음원을 듣고 받아쓰는 연습을 통해 Listening 능력 또한 향상

English Spectrum 1, 2

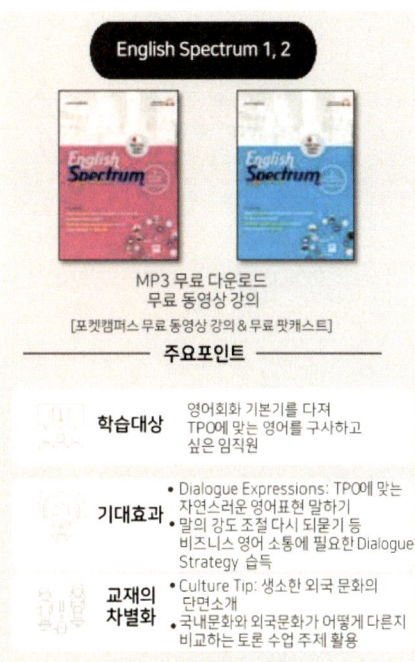

MP3 무료 다운로드
무료 동영상 강의
[포켓캠퍼스 무료 동영상 강의 & 무료 팟캐스트]

주요포인트

학습대상	영어회화 기본기를 다져 TPO에 맞는 영어를 구사하고 싶은 임직원
기대효과	• Dialogue Expressions: TPO에 맞는 자연스러운 영어표현 말하기 • 말의 강도 조절 다시 되묻기 등 비즈니스 영어 소통에 필요한 Dialogue Strategy 습득
교재의 차별화	• Culture Tip: 생소한 외국 문화의 단면소개 • 국내문화와 외국문화가 어떻게 다른지 비교하는 토론 수업 주제 활용

비즈니스 파이오니어 1, 2

MP3 무료 다운로드
무료 동영상 강의

주요포인트

학습대상	비지니스 영어 실력 향상 및 체계적인 비즈니스 영어표현이 필요한 임직원
기대효과	글로벌 소통이 필요할 때 필요한 직장인/오피스 필수 영어 표현익히기
교재의 차별화	교재가 영어로 구성 Socializing, telephoning, presentation 등 전반적인 핵심 표현 정리

비즈니스 인터엑션
(미팅, 프리젠테이션, 이메일)

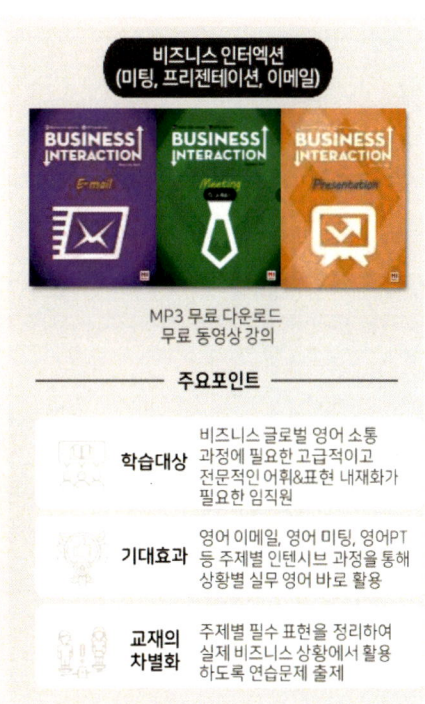

MP3 무료 다운로드
무료 동영상 강의

주요포인트

학습대상	비즈니스 글로벌 영어 소통 과정에 필요한 고급적이고 전문적인 어휘&표현 내재화가 필요한 임직원
기대효과	영어 이메일, 영어 미팅, 영어PT 등 주제별 인텐시브 과정을 통해 상황별 실무 영어 바로 활용
교재의 차별화	주제별 필수 표현을 정리하여 실제 비즈니스 상황에서 활용 하도록 연습문제 출제